FUN WITH GROWING HERBS INDOORS

Virginie F. and George A. Elbert

Photographs by the authors

Crown Publishers, Inc.   New York

For Suzanne
with love from
Jinny and George

Inquiries should be addressed to Crown Publishers, Inc., 419 Park Avenue South, New York, N.Y. 10016

Library of Congress Catalog Card Number: 74–80320
Printed in the United States of America
Published simultaneously in Canada by
General Publishing Company Limited
Designed by Nedda Balter

Contents

ACKNOWLEDGMENTS

We are deeply grateful for the assistance of:
T. H. Everett of the New York Botanical Garden
for the photographs on pages 88, 90, 103, 106,
110, 116, 121, 122, and 179
and Peter Ruh of Sunnybrook Farm Nursery

I

All about Herbs

THE INDOOR HERB GARDENER

Indoor herb gardening is quite a new art and interest which is becoming immensely popular because it offers to our increasingly urban style of living a way of counteracting the sterility of the environment. While herb gardening outdoors attracts about the same number of devotees as formerly, members of the new generation have enthusiastically taken to it indoors. Most of them live in crowded suburbs or in apartments with no means of gardening in the open. Quite spontaneously they have evinced a craving to have living plants around them.

Through herbs they discover a whole world of plants that are not only decorative greenery but offer fragrant or aromatic flowers and leaves, some of which are also commonly used in cooking. We see this as the second stage in the inevitable invasion of the home by gardens. The final stage, already practiced by many, is the growing of flowering plants. Ultimately the indoor garden will include many more different kinds of plants than we have ever known in gardens of any sort before.

At this stage, the greatest stumbling block to successful herb gardening indoors is the unquestioning acceptance of tradition. All that has been done for a long time is to select a few of the herbs grown in outdoor gardens and grow them in the home. But that is only a beginning. Our indoor environment is totally different and permits us to exploit a far wider range of plant material.

We have inherited our herb tradition from northern Europe, especially from England. Because the climate of England is much milder than ours, we have been forced to limit our growing still further. In the northern parts of the United States our choices have become fewer and fewer.

Herbs grow all over the world, in every climate, but we have come to think of them as plants only of a certain kind—those that flourish in the harsh north and tolerate long months of frost. Normal tropical herbs have been passed off as greenhouse plants or ignored as "not hardy." Even the herbs of Mediterranean countries, whence many of the most important ones were adapted to English conditions, are treated as curiosities since they cannot be grown in "official" herb gardens. The exclusivity of herb gardening goes even further. All the many medicinal and aromatic herbs that do not happen to grow well in ordinary garden loam in full sun are banished, and hardly a shrub is included in the herbalist's canon.

So we find that, unless we repeat ourselves endlessly, we must change our whole point of view in order to make indoor herb gardening an exciting adventure. Our indoor "climate" is mild and adaptable. Thousands of herb plants which could not survive a northern winter will flourish in the home. All we have to do is to pick and choose those that are most pleasant, most useful, and that cause us the least amount of trouble to grow well. Since the number of possibilities is so vast, it will take some time before we have explored even the most obvious ones. So, our book, made up partly of old and partly of new herbs (as far as the standard herb garden is concerned), is only a beginning and an encouragement to continue on your own.

Some of our choices of plants for indoor herb growing may surprise you. For they may run counter to what you have come to consider a herb. We are so conditioned to a few repeated and repeated lists of cookery herbs—or quaint medicinals—that it may come as a shock to find that many plants which we already grow in the garden or the home are officially herbs. And to these must be added the beginnings of a wider repertory—the wonderful and inexhaustible treasures of tropical herbs.

Herb growing starts with the realization that many of those commonly used in cooking can live indoors. The idea of using fresh, home-grown plants to flavor food is endlessly appealing. Having them in the kitchen provides a sense of the outdoors, and we feel that it is a way of avoiding the artificial flavors that are associated with chemical additives in food and pollution of the environment.

As plants that have a direct effect on the human organism and on our senses, herbs have played an important role in the history of mankind. They are intimately connected with religion, myth, legend, and, of course, medicine in all the world's cultures. They continue to exert an influence far beyond what we might expect in so scientific an age as ours. Learning about their qualities, their uses, and their histories is an important aspect of their fascination. But, even if none of these subjects arouses your curiosity, you will have fun growing herbs indoors.

HOW TO PRONOUNCE HERB

In England the aitch is strongly aspirated. Most Americans have been taught to say 'erb, much as the cockney says 'enry—a classical example of reversed English. Recently those in the know here have been copying the English pronunciation and almost cough when they give forth with the aitch, just to be sure everyone hears it right. In the long run, we suppose, the English way will prevail. However, as long as you don't say 'oib, you won't be ostracized from polite society.

WHAT'S A HERB?

In botany a herb is a flowering plant whose stem above ground does not become woody. That includes, of course, among others, our usual garden flowers and the vegetables. The herbalist's definition is quite different. It is any plant valued for its *medicinal properties, flavor, or scent.* That knocks out the botanical restriction entirely. Quite a few ferns and other primitive plants that do not flower arc included in herbal medicine. Although the classical herb garden of Europe and America contains mostly plants that are botanically herbaceous, there are innumerable shrubs and trees that fit the herbalist's definition. Furthermore, we find that some plants which have other uses, for instance dyeing materials, have found their way into herb gardens. Where to draw the line at all becomes a vexing problem which herb writers have solved by ducking the issue entirely.

Long experience with plants and plant literature convinces us that most growing things have been used medicinally at some time in history, somewhere in the world. There is hardly a mention of a plant in the old literature that does not associate it with some imagined or real curative property. Culinary and fragrant herbs are fewer in number but every region of the world has its own. So we end up with the opinion that the traditional European herb garden is very limited indeed.

Nevertheless, we also note that modern outdoor herb gardeners have completely followed their fancy and, within the extremely broad lines we have drawn, will grow any plant to which, by the most far-fetched conclusions, they can attribute any herbal qualities. In the end it has come down really to the tastes and interests of the individual and the soil and climate of the garden.

The matter of definition is rather important for us because growing herbs indoors is something quite new. And we don't want to be accused by the experts of having overstepped reasonable bounds. In practice we find that the American outdoor herb gardener is even more restricted by his climate than the English, raising a rather small list of the most common and easiest-to-grow plants. Most of these are culinary herbs.

In many respects the indoor gardening environment is more favorable and permits a far greater range of plant material. For, in addition to the herbs of the temperate zones of Europe and America, which are the usual ones, he can explore those from the subtropics and tropics which are innumerable. So don't be concerned because you are *only* an indoor grower. You have your handicaps too, but can grow just as much a variety as the outdoor herb gardener.

herb (ûrb, hûrb), *n.* **1.** a flowering plant whose stem above ground does not become woody. **2.** such a plant when valued for its medicinal properties, flavor, scent, or the like. **3.** *Archaic.* herbage. [ME *herbe* < OF *erbe, herbe* < L *herb(a)*] —**herb'less.** *adj.* —**herb'like'.** *adj.*

Definitions of *herbs, herbaceous,* and so on. From the Random House Dictionary, College Edition.

HOW HERBS ARE USED

Leaves, bark, roots, flowers, and seeds of herbs are used in a variety of ways. From flowers and leaves essential oils for the perfume industry are distilled. Leaves, bark, and roots are boiled or distilled to extract their medicinal elements. Seeds supply flavoring and medicine. Roots, not cultivated for nourishment alone, are usually medicinal if rated as herbs. Some herbs are grown simply for their living fragrance of flower or leaf.

Bay or laurel leaves, a stem of dried Grecian sage (*Salvia officinalis*), cinnamon bark, cardamon and anise seeds, and a bottle of horse radish, scraped from the roots of *Armoracia rusticana*, are examples of parts of plants used herbally. To these must be added fragrant blossoms used in perfume and for fragrance in the home.

The purpose of this book is to show how herbs can be grown and displayed in the home—a subject quite large enough to fill our pages without padding, as is the custom, with bits and pieces of information regarding the various myths, legends, and uses. Hundreds of books have been written on each aspect and some of these are listed in the bibliography. Should you wish to delve deeper into ancient herbal lore there is plenty of published material for you to study.

CATEGORIES OF PLANTS

Herbaceous Plants. Many herbal plants also conform to the botanist's definition. In fact these comprise most of the herbs in the traditional gardens. Their growth is the same as that of standard garden flowers except that they are valued for different reasons. Typical herbaceous herbs that we grow in the herb garden are most of the daisy, mint, and all the carrot family. These are all soft-stemmed plants. Bulbous herbs are also herbaceous.

Shrubs. Box is a good example of a true herb shrub. But many plants that are soft when young develop woodiness with age. The rose is really a shrub, and old rosemary plants look like bonsaied forest trees or topiary. The outdoor herb gardener raises many of the smaller shrubby plants and occasionally some larger ones. Indoors it is a matter of space and size. Large specimens can often be grown on the sun porch or near a sunny window. The tropical plant repertory is particularly rich in shrubs with aromatic leaves or perfumed flowers which are a delight in the house.

Trees. It is well known that *Salix,* the willow, was since time immemorial the source of a pain-killer that, in modern times, has been synthesized as acetylsalicylic acid and marketed as aspirin. Sassafras is an important herb tree, as are cinchona and coffee. Examples of American herbal trees are yellow chestnut, the tag alder, the sweet birch, the blue or hornbeam water beech, and the fringe tree. None of these is grown in the outdoor herb garden and they are unsuitable for the house. However indoors has it all over outdoors in the matter of herbal trees, for young tropical herbal trees do very well in the house. Young tamarinds and coffee trees are examples of trees that have only recently been grown indoors. Orange, lemon, and kumquat trees have long been popular. They and dwarf pomegranates produce flower and fruit. There is a whole world of juvenile trees for the herbal gardener to explore, many of which cannot even be mentioned here for lack of space. Incidentally, many of the trees are far more attractive as pot plants than the popular avocado tree and, with many Caribbean fruits coming into the market, the indoor herb grower has a supply of seed right at hand. Here the indoor grower has all the best of it.

Bulbs and Roots. The onions are all technically herbs and ginger root makes an interesting houseplant. A famous root herb is ginseng. *Panax quinquefolium* is the American source. We do not know whether it will grow indoors but you might try. It is a common woodland spring flower. The problem with most root herbs is that they require a deep soil or are very large plants above ground so that very few are grown in the indoor garden.

A herbal tree, *Quercus rubra,* the red oak. "An old remedy for diarrhoea. The acorns are grated or powdered and washed down with water." The bark was used as an astringent externally as it contains a large amount of tannin. The illustration is from John Torrey's *A Flora of the State of New York,* Vol. II 1843.

Panax quinquefolium, American ginseng. This is so valued a medicinal herb in the Far East that the botanist Kalm could report around 1750 that Canadian Indians were gathering it in quantities to sell to merchants in Montreal and Quebec for shipment abroad. The plant, formerly common in the wild, has now become rare and the demand still persists. The root, which is shown in the drawing, is the valuable part. From Britton & Brown *Illustrated Flora* 1913.

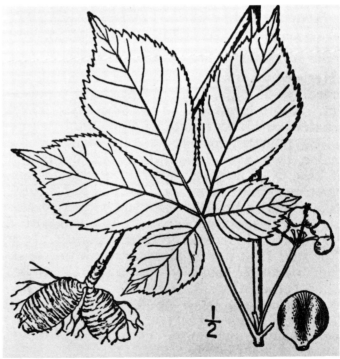

SPECIAL HERB INTERESTS

For Culinary Use. Herb cooking has come into great repute and popularity ever since the preparation of meat and fish stocks for sauces became unacceptable labor, to say nothing of the expense. Flavoring with herbs has replaced them and brought new life into the kitchen. Most grocery stores now display a respectable selection, dried and packaged.

The plants themselves fit nicely in the kitchen window or beneath the cabinet on the worktable under fluorescent light. Even the most sterile culinary environment gets a lift from a herbal garden. Almost all indoor herb gardening starts with kitchen herbs.

Of course, if you want to cook with them, don't consult a herb book. There are excellent cooks who know how to grow herbs. But the herbalist who is a good cook is rarer than truffles. The recipes whipped up are awful beyond belief. Using very large quantities of herbs in cooking is bad practice in the first place and requires a big supply of plants. An exception, because she is both herbalist and superb cook, is Milo Miloradovich's *The Art of Cooking with Herbs and Spices* (Doubleday). This is a classic on the subject and doesn't confuse fairy tales with cooking.

We suppose that, under culinary herbal preparations, we should include those teas that are taken more for pleasure than as medicine. They are without number and some of our herb-loving friends have been making all kinds of witches' brews and going into ecstasies over them. There are chamomile, lime flower, mint, and geranium teas. Alas, we love herbs, but we love real tea best. That's an herb too and quite a good houseplant to boot. As a change, a cup of herb tea may be amusing but we doubt it will ever become a truly popular beverage. Growing some of these plants, on the other hand, is fun.

The basic culinary herbs are basil, the mints, chives and shallots, origanum, marjoram, rosemary, savory, sage, thyme, tarragon, and parsley—all standard in the outdoor garden.

Fragrant Herbs. A collection of sweet or pungent-smelling herbs may well be the interest of a herb gardener. In the Mediterranean region, when the low-growing scrub, called maquis in French and macchia in Italian, is at its height of growth and blooming in the spring, the air is laden with the balsamic odors of myrrh, rosemary, and thyme. Wherever you walk in it, the plants you tread under foot exhale an aroma so strong as to make you dizzy. Sailors sense the hot sun fragrance of it many miles at sea.

You will not have this experience in your herb garden, indoors or out. The best you can expect, except from a few fragrant flowers, is that leaves, when rubbed, will emit a rich or pungent odor.

Modern herbalists have not insisted that the fragrant herbs all be of the kind used in perfume. They seem to grow any plant that has aromatic or perfumed leaves or flowers to their liking. We cannot do better than emulate them. Rose petals and geranium leaves add aroma and some flavor to apple and other jellies that sometimes are tasteless in themselves. For some the most interesting plants of this group are those that emit an odor so incongruous as to constitute a conversation piece. The surprise of a visitor who rubs the leaves of pineapple sage or the curry plant is its own reward.

We find the presence of aromatic herbs most rewarding. Though the air is not noticeably heavy laden with their combined odors, they do counteract the mustiness of the house and the polluted air of the city. There *is* a difference in the air of a home that has fragrant herbs growing—even though it be only a clean outdoorsy smell. And, with a flick of a finger you can stir up a perfume that clears the head of the urban stagnation. An added bonus is the sense of collecting fragrances, an adventure in the sense of smell which herbs offer over anything else that can be grown in the home. As we come to know the tropical plants better, among which are so many with rich and spicy odors, this branch of herb gardening will become more and more popular.

American Herbs. Most of the herbs grown in outdoor herb gardens continue to be of northern European origin. This is not because Europe had the better species to begin with but that the plants have been cultivated and selected there for centuries and become much superior to the wild plants. English herbs in particular have been cultivated in our gardens but some of them, proving too tender for our severe winters and summers, have been replaced by native American relatives.

When the European settlers arrived here, they found that the Indians had a complete herbal lore of their own based on the native plants. And since, in the early stages at least, the herbs to which they were accustomed in their homelands were unavailable, the Dutch, Germans, English, and Swedes used the local products which were gathered in the wild.

Some modern herbal gardeners find it amusing to collect and plant the American equivalents of the European herbal canon. In *The Herbalist,* a popular medicinal herbal by Joseph E. Meyer, the uses of many of the American herbs are recorded. There are any number of books on the subject of Indian herbal remedies. Some of these plants do very well in the garden. In fact a number must be classed as weeds, or noxious plants, in a cultivated garden, while others are quite well behaved. The names given to some of these plants by the pioneers, such as rattlesnake bane, fleabane, fly poison, birthwort, Culver's physic, heartsease, and nerve root are so amusing as to make growing them almost worthwhile for this reason alone. However, very few are useful to the indoor gardener because so many are either deciduous or need a long freezing period between seasonal growths.

Legendary Herbs. Not all herb growers are interested either in the use or appearance of plants. Some are attracted rather by their mythology. Throughout the ages magic powers have been attributed to some, while others have been identified with real or legendary heroes. There is also a regular cult of herbal symbolism. Robert Graves, in *The White Goddess* and other books, has written fascinating speculations on these matters. For instance he relates the Druidic sign language code to very ancient identifications of herbs as symbols for letters and for prehistoric events and mythology. A gardener may well plant examples of this type for their suggestions of the language of art, myth, or poetry.

The Doctrine of Signatures. Formerly it was believed that the deity placed all creatures on earth for a specific purpose—mostly or entirely for the benefit of man. It was essential in the search for knowledge that mankind learn the hidden intentions and discover the virtues residing in every living creature. One of the clues that revealed these virtues was the form imparted to the animal or plant.

Thus, since the leaves of pulmonaria were shaped like a lung, it was obvious that the plant was good for bronchial conditions and was therefore called lungwort. A plant with a swollen aboveground tuber might be good for gout. A high incidence of unemployment is reported for such plants nowadays. Those possessing leaves with heavy veining, similar to a snake's skin, would act against the venom. Certain plants were related by appearance to the signs of the zodiac. So medieval and Renaissance herb doctors tied their use to astrology. . . . the conjunction of a zodiacal period and their use being considered efficacious.

This was the Doctrine of Signatures. Herbal writers like to believe that it really came into use during the Middle Ages in Europe. But, as a matter of fact, all primitive people have drawn similar conclusions without having any familiarity with European writers.

The doctrine has proved, of course, the least reliable indicator of medicinal or other effects. But there are those who, for fun or because they have a penchant for this sort of mysticism, still collect such herbs —and some still believe in the theory.

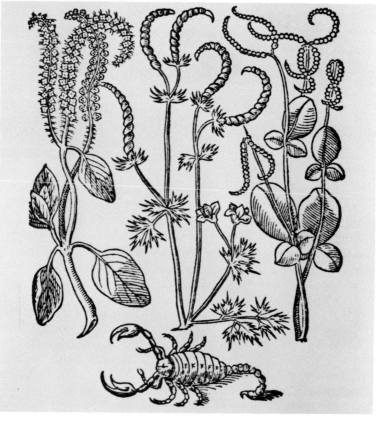

Herbs associated with the zodiacal sign of the Scorpion. Giambattista Porta 1591 *Phytognomonica.* A fancied relationship of herbs to astrological signs matched the equally imaginary identification of the signs with heavenly bodies and their influence on man.

Herbs for Color or Texture. It has often been noted that the colors of a herb garden are grey and green. Grey, including silvery, velvety, and fuzzy, is a rarer color in plants than green. Hence, in choosing a contrast for the formal herb gardens, color and texture of leaves, plus a tight mounded habit, became more important than their usefulness. The herbal gardener salves his conscience, if necessary, by growing some plants of this kind that are close relatives of the real herbs. In this way he can indulge in those formal patterns of mounded and clipped plants that are so much a part of the herb cult. A foliage garden is the result.

Quite a number of such herbs are quite attractive for indoor growing. It can easily be argued that, since the crop of useful herbs indoors is inevitably minuscule, it is more fun to grow a pretty plant which is useless than a sprawler without charm which does not produce enough leaves for the pot or salad to make it worthwhile.

Medicinal Herbs. By far the most important use for herbs has been in medicine and many more plants are listed in this category than any other. We need no better evidence that modern herb growing is more aesthetic than practical than the absence of medicinals from gardens. Some culinary and aromatic herbs are also medicinal but only the specialist cares about that aspect. And, though the lore is altogether fascinating and complex, we mention it here only briefly because, while it has played so large a part in the history of herb gardening, modern interest has fallen off considerably.

Long before the dawn of history, men must have been using herbs to cure their ailments. While searching for food, especially at times of epidemic or famine, they tried out different leaves, fruits, seeds, and roots which were not part of their ordinary diet. These experiments led to the discovery that certain plants had some effect in relieving their afflictions. Over the centuries a very substantial body of remedies was accumulated, some real, some imaginary. The search was universal, for there is no primitive people on earth that has not found in its clime and soil some useful medicinal plants. Even today herbal medicine is prevalent wherever modern science has not penetrated or where modern remedies are too expensive.

Many herbal remedies have been dropped from the pharmacopoeias as ineffective, too limited in supply, or downright dangerous in use. But a very great number are still retained, and scientific medicine continues its search into the medicinal qualities of plants, attempting to isolate and synthesize the chemical structures that are responsible for their particular effects on the human system.

Modern medicine, if not infallible, is pretty clear about its distinctions. Unfortunately the herb cultist is not: he gets his myth, his magic, his history, and his medicine all mixed up, so that one never knows whether he is dealing with something useful or something worthless or worse. Half-truths are sufficient to convince most people and, spiced with a good story, account for the addiction of many to the fallacies as well as the truths. The only reliable guide to the use of herbs is a modern official pharmacopoeia.

A relatively few amateurs still grow medicinal herbs these days. Most people know too little about their uses and distrust them. If they pick out the more attractive ones for growing, they will usually find that they are included already in some other category—among the fragrant or culinary plants. The medicinal herb garden therefore mainly survives in public places as a demonstration of the ancient knowledge and method. It is true that "organic medicine" enjoys a vogue along with "organic food," but most of the cultists would rather buy their herbs than grow them.

Nevertheless, for the indoor gardener, medicinal herbs may offer a host of interesting plants from the warmer parts of the world—sometimes trees and bushes—which can be grown into very acceptable houseplants and bring with them the glamour of a strange name, an exotic habitat, or an interesting use. It may encourage us to try plants that otherwise would not be considered because of the unlikelihood of our growing them to a size or condition that will provide flower and fruit. These plants may prove to be most interesting specimens as juveniles. And sometimes we may get blossoms and can triumphantly display the fruits. Many of these plants produce leaves or flowers that are aromatic or fragrant and will complement our traditional herbs.

2

A Ridiculously Short History of Herbals and Herb Gardens

The history of herbals and herb gardens is a fascinating subject but of no obvious practical value for the indoor gardener. However, readers who are inspired to pursue the matter further may find that this enrichment of their knowledge will spur them on to try different plants from those we include in our cultural list and may even suggest ways of arranging growing herbs in the confines of a house. With whole room gardens a practical reality due to fluorescent light, the herb gardens of the past may yet be reproduced indoors.

The First "Modern" Herbal. For thousands of years the Egyptians, Chinese, Indians, and Mesopotamians collected herbs for medicine and magic and recorded their uses. The Greeks and Romans were equally active, had the beginnings of medical schools, and employed herbs in their systems. But the first lasting work on the subject, *De Materia Medica,* was compiled by a Roman physician in Nero's army, named Dioscorides, in the first century A.D. The manuscript, which listed 600 medicinal plants, was copied and referred to for fifteen centuries as an authority as basic as Aristotle for philosophy or Galen for medicine. Later editions of his work were illustrated by various artists with fanciful or realistic drawings of the plants.

Monastic Gardens. During the barbarian invasions of southern Europe, systematic agriculture and, of course, gardening virtually disappeared. The revival began with the gardens established by Saint Benedict in the sixth century at the monastery of Monte Cassino. His order sought to make the monks self-supporting in the matter of food. In addition to the cultivation of staple foods, an orchard and a herb garden were laid out and served as models for other monastic foundations. In such herb gardens Dioscorides' list was generally followed.

Sonchus sp. From a Dioscorides Codex of the early sixth century A.D. Medieval drawings of plants did not compare with these much earlier efforts.

Ferula sp. An illustration from a Dioscorides Codex, early sixth century A.D.

A late medieval garden. The beds are rectangular, raised, and faced with wood or brick. In order not to confuse the design artists of the period drew in very few plants. This has been misinterpreted by modern writers as an indication that plants were not raised in quantity in such formal arrangements. Crisp, *Medieval Gardens.* (Hacker.)

The plantings were usually in rectangular raised beds confined by low plank or brick facings. It was almost another thousand years before the basic design and content of a herb garden was changed.

In modern times imitations of monastic herb gardens have been planted and maintained in a number of places in the Western World. There is a fine example at the Cloisters in New York.

Botanical Gardens. The first botanical gardens were those of Pisa and Padua. The Orto Botanico in Padua was established in 1545 and has been preserved in its essentials. The purpose was to supply the medical faculty of the university with examples of herbs for teaching and medicine. The layout is an exquisite design and a very practical way of displaying the plants.

The Great Herbalists and Knot Gardens. In the sixteenth and seventeenth centuries herbal "science" was greatly expanded and the cult became extremely popular. It is from the sixteenth century that the most beautiful woodcut illustrations, in publications by Fuchs, Matthioli, and Brunfels, have come down to us. At the same time such herbalists as Culpeper, Gerard, and Turner enjoyed a great vogue for their cures, combining herbal medicine, astrology, and other forms of mysticism. The modern cultist gets a great kick out of this old lore and not infrequently even comes to believe in it literally. It is from their works, rather than from the beginning scientists, that most of the lectures on herbs and the texts of many books are drawn.

At this time knot gardens became fashionable. No more demanding, costly, and troublesome method of gardening was ever invented. For it involved growing and training plants into ropelike mounds which seemed to snake across each other, over and under, without interruption. The different strands consisted of herbs in contrasting shades of grey and green and the effect was undoubtedly very stylish and handsome. The spaces between the strands contained relatively few plants, design being more important than color or the "crop." Even contemporaries ridiculed a style that demanded inhuman efforts to maintain. So the fad lasted only a relatively short time. A few knot gardens are still grown as a historical record.

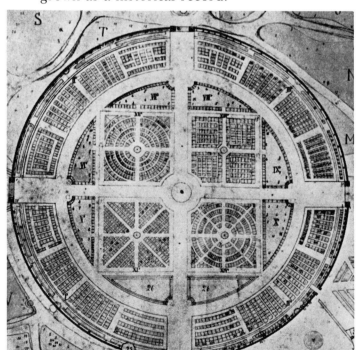

Design of the Orto Botanico at Padua. The layout is unchanged today. The circular area is set below the level of the corners providing a superb view of the neat raised beds with their small specimen plants.

Looking down to the center of the Orto Botanico at Padua. No more handsome and harmonious design has ever been conceived.

Design for a knot garden. The "ropes" were made with low hedges of slow-growing plants. There was not much room for planting in such a design and, in fact, the spaces were often left empty. Crisp, *Medieval Gardens.* (Hacker.)

Design for a maze. The same means were used as in knot gardens. Solving the maze was no problem as the hedges were so low that anyone could step over them. When a child, one of us got lost in the maze at Hampton Court and had to be rescued by the guard. No excuse, but the hedges were at least man high . . . a later development.

Parterre Gardens. In the seventeenth century the Italians and French took the lead with parterre gardens. This was a much more important contribution to garden design—one that has lasted up to the present day and is represented in most formal garden plantings. The method was used not only for the planting of herbs but wherever gardens were laid out with flowers.

The parterre consisted of perfectly clipped hedges, planted and trained in designs similar to the embroidery of the period, each block being divided by paths from the others. Some of these gardens have no flowers at all, the open spaces being covered with carefully raked sand. In others a mass of low-growing blooming flowers provides color. In the herb gardens spaces in the design were filled with specimens of different varieties and the hedges were usually lower, giving more prominence to the plants. Also the hedges themselves were often composed of herbal plants.

Originally these gardens, essentially without shade, were meant not to walk about in spring or summer but to be seen from the upper-story windows of the palace or house from which they stretched out like an extension of the living room rug.

Magnificent examples of these gardens have been preserved in England, France, and Italy. At the Château de Villandry, in France, there is a reconstruction of unique magnificence. The flower parterres are all based on the design of a heart, but each is different. Paths between the squares consist of sand raked in a pattern. The kitchen gardens are extensive, the borders low and geometric. Arbors and small trained trees are set at the corners for decoration and shade.

The general idea of the parterre has persisted in even the most ordinary modern civic garden plantings. Sometimes we see begonias, for instance, used as a temporary edging, instead of the more permanent, slow-growing shrubs. Parterre herb gardens are maintained by some commercial nurseries and by garden clubs.

The immense parterre gardens at the Château de Villandry, France, a reconstruction of a seventeenth century garden. On the lower level are the kitchen and herb gardens which are as formal in their design as the rest. An immense amount of labor is required to keep such a garden in mint condition. For this reason these are among the wonders of the world. Notice the shrubs and the arbors. The parterre designs on the upper level are all variations on the form of the heart. *Photo by the authors.*

Modern Herb Gardens. In more recent times it has become fashionable to use the parterre method and plant in whimsical or humorous shapes. There are herb gardens designed as clockfaces, like sundials, in the signs of the zodiac, wheel spokes or butterflies. Caprilands Herb Farm at Coventry, Connecticut, includes in its herb listings a design for a butterfly herb garden. The variety of plants listed, however, is quite small considering the complexity of the design. The herb garden at the Cleveland Garden Centre, maintained by the Western Reserve Herb Society, is one in the best traditions of the art. It includes all the best of the techniques and shows the contrasting forms and leaves to best advantage.

Indoor Applications. The indoor growing of a great variety of herbs is so new that little has been done to adapt garden designs to the home. We believe that in bay windows, on sun porches, in garden rooms, and even on trays some of the aspects of the parterre effect can be produced in miniature. Thus far we have not engaged in testing our theories but we invite others to consider it. Herbs lend themselves to miniaturization and the greys and greens so prominently worked into the design of outdoor herb gardens can certainly be carried out indoors with some ingenuity and skill.

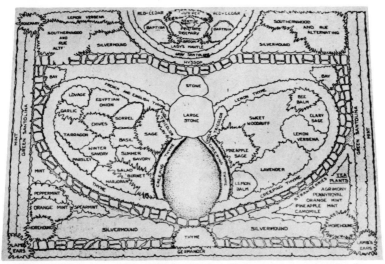

A "butterfly" herb garden. The herbs are all decorative or hardy plants, confined to relatively few species. *Courtesy, Caprilands Herb Farm, North Coventry, Conn.*

Modern herb garden maintained by the Western Reserve Herb Society at the Garden Center of Greater Cleveland. This is the finest planting we have seen in America. A perfect blend of spaciousness, design, and contrasting textures of beautifully groomed plants. The low tight growth shows what can be achieved partly in the house by training plants to show the maximum amount of leafage in the smallest space and shaping in a pleasing way.

Magnificent topiary herbs from the greenhouses of Mrs. Paul Mellon. The three large plants in front are Santolinas. The short tree behind the tall santolina on the left is a curry plant *(Helichrysum angustifolium).* The trees to the right, of which only the tops can be seen, are thyme. Smaller editions of these uniquely trained plants are possible, grown on a windowsill, if carefully trained.
Photograph by Mr. Joseph H. Bailey, courtesy Mrs. Paul Mellon.

Miracles of training with basil plants, here shown in four sizes, from Mrs. Paul Mellon's greenhouses. The progression shows how the small one can develop into the fine shrub in the center.
Photograph by Mr. Joseph H. Bailey, courtesy Mrs. Paul Mellon.

3

Annual, Biennial, and Perennial Plants

As you may well be a beginner with plants such as herbs, which do not all just keep growing like the tropical foliage plants you buy from the florist, and since we will be using the terms in our text, it may be useful to give a few definitions.

Annual Plants. They complete their life cycle in a single season. In the process they produce seed, which comes up the following year or awaits a favorable opportunity. Seed from tropical plants will sprout if planted shortly after ripening. Some come up within a few days after planting, while others may take months before showing above ground. Seed from plants that are accustomed to a freezing winter usually will not germinate unless they are subjected to a period of extreme cold.

Thus there is a difference between seed you gather yourself in the North and that sold by seedsmen. The latter can be planted at any time since, if they require a cold spell, they have been subjected to it before being shipped to you. Seedsmen, however, usually avoid handling cold-spell seeds. If you gather such seeds yourself, you can place them in the refrigerator (not in the freezer compartment) for six to eight weeks. They will then be viable.

The life cycle of annual plants requires that they produce seed, many of which need not be planted immediately but will last a long time in a dry state. Investigators have found seeds that germinated after lying dormant for thousands of years. However there are quite a few that quickly lose their viability. Angelica, an herb too big to grow indoors advantageously, has seeds that must be planted within a few months at most after ripening. Old packets of seed, therefore, may or may not germinate. Seedsmen do, however, usually place a date on the package that tells you how long you can keep the seeds.

Fortunately most of the herbs that do well indoors are perennials.

However, if you do want to grow one of the annual herbs you will usually find it necessary to start with seed because the nurseries carry very few of them as plants, have still fewer in pots, and transplanting is very risky.

Since annual plants rarely last out the year in the house, we must sow seeds at intervals in order to have continuous foliage or bloom indoors.

Another point to note is that annuals are usually sun lovers and do not take kindly to the lower illumination indoors. Their need to reach the light quickly in order to bloom and seed has resulted in their possessing relatively long stems with little branching near the ground. Those with leaves on the ground develop tall flowering stalks. These growth patterns make some of them quite unsuitable for indoor growing.

Biennial Plants. Biennials are those that complete part of their growth in one year and then flower and produce seed in the second year, completing their life cycle. In the house most biennials produce flowers in the first year. However, two years is about as long a time as you can keep them going. Eventually they become woody and play themselves out.

Perennial Plants. Perennials have a normal life cycle of more than two years and, once mature, produce flower and seed every year. Some reach flowering size in a single year while others may take many years. Perennials of the temperate and cold zones lose their leaves in the fall. Herbaceous plants of this type die down to the ground, only the roots staying alive through the winter. Of these there are two types. One, from the more northern regions, will die unless subjected to a lengthy period of subfreezing weather. The others, from more southern regions, may tolerate both conditions, staying green continuously if the weather is sufficiently warm in winter. The latter type of plant, among the herbs, is particularly useful to the indoor grower because it usually belongs to a species which has a number of transitional forms. If the indoor herb grower selects a plant requiring freezing, he will lose it in due time. But if he chooses a plant which can tolerate the warmth of the house throughout the year he has one which usually behaves in all essential ways like a tropical plant.

Tropical plants usually remain green throughout the year. Some do lose their leaves and they may even bloom on the bare branches but all our houseplants are of the first type. All in all, the tender herbs from southern regions are those that grow best in the house.

Nurserymen carry many more different kinds of perennial than annual herbs. And it is a big advantage to buy the plants rather than to grow from seed, for you then have the opportunity to judge the growth habit and test the fragrance or aroma. If you like the plant it can be multiplied vegetatively. However, if you want to experiment with some of the interesting tropical shrubs and trees you may be obliged to use seed since plants may be unavailable.

Bulbs and Tubers. These root or stem thickenings serve to store water just as does the leafless globe form of a cactus. The plants from northern climates go dormant during periods of cold and dryness, while those from the tropics die down in the warm dry season and revive with the rains. The situation is similar to that described for other perennial plants. There are some bulbs that will only sprout, once they have died down, if they are subjected to a period of cold. Others, from tropical regions, usually have a habit of inactivity for a definite time period. At the end of the period, whether water is applied or not, they begin to sprout. When that happens, if not moistened within a short time they will continue to grow and exhaust all the moisture and nourishment in the tuber.

Among the bulbous herbs there are only a few that require a winter freeze. Those that do can be placed in the refrigerator for eight weeks in a dry state. Returned to warmth and moistened, they will start to sprout. Lily of the valley pips, for instance, require this freezing period.

4

Where to Grow Your Herbs Indoors

Most homes do not provide sufficient space to grow the amount of herbs required for constant kitchen use. A small crop of rosemary will do because it is so very pungent. But most of the other herbs must be considered a supplement. We grow many of the culinary herbs because they are not merely useful but are ornamental in a different way from our other houseplants.

Sun porches are not that common anymore. Lean-to and window greenhouses have increased in number but are rarely used for growing herbs. Windowsill areas are small. A basement garden or a section of living room given over to a herb garden provides a fair harvest. But most people use shelving or three-tier carts for their artificial light growing.

For most of us one, two, or three pots of any one herb is about the limit. And if we want to grow a great number of different herbs our pots must be small. Visitors to our herb-growing area are astonished at the smallness of our pots. The plants do very well nevertheless and we like it that way. It isn't ideal but it permits us to have variety in this amusing category of plants.

Whole rooms are being turned into artificial light gardens these days and, no doubt, a quite substantial crop can be grown in them. But very few will be able to afford this luxury for some time to come. It is hardly worth considering for average growers. Grow your herbs for pleasure and for some, but not very great, use. The fun is in the growing, the seeing, the smelling, and the tasting.

Space considerations also affect our choices of herbs to grow. An angelica, which reaches five or more feet in a single season, does not make an ideal houseplant. And though we can raise ornamental shrubs or trees in tubs, the number we have room for is limited. We are more successful if we prune such plants and maintain them as dwarfs. Low herbs do well under fluorescent light but the moment we try tall ones we run into trouble. Therefore, except for a few specimen plants for the sun porch or a position near a window, most of our choices must be confined to those which are reasonably compact, spreading a foot and a half at most and reaching a height of not more than two feet. We will be able to have much more variety and pleasure from herbs if we keep them small.

Scale. The choice of smaller plants for the house is also dictated by the matter of differences in scale.

In a garden we look down on the plants that are below eye level and straight ahead at the tall ones, like delphiniums and dahlias. Of the half-high plants we see only the clusters of flowers at the top and are hardly ever conscious of the long bare stems below. When small plants, such as lobelias and candytuft, are grown in the border, we crowd them together to get an effect of mass—otherwise they would look utterly insignificant. These phenomena of scale are the result of comparison with trees and buildings out of doors.

Indoors the scale is much smaller. We see the plants close up. The relative size of small plants and furniture is about the same as garden plants compared with trees and houses. A dahlia plant looks monstrous in this environment and little plants become much more important.

For our purposes the point is that small herbs will look better in the house than out-of-doors. They are no longer lost as individuals in the crowd and we can enjoy their natural forms. Long-stemmed plants, such as so many of the members of the *Umbelliferae,* or carrot family, look ungainly, while very large, coarse plants have no place in our indoor herb garden. On the other hand daily attention to our smaller plants gives us the opportunity to train and groom them. Many are capable of being shaped into formal designs which can last for years— especially the small shrubby kinds.

These limitations of scale will become more understandable when we select plants for indoor growing and will explain why some quite popular herbs for the outdoor garden are left out.

A few pots of herbs bring cheer to a city windowsill. The large plant on the left is *Lavandula dentata* (lavender) and the one on the right is a rosemary.

Matters of scale also influence our attitude toward the flowers of herbs. In the garden most of the herbal inflorescences are no more attractive than those of any weed. But indoors the small clusters of bloom are very welcome and attractive. For this reason, although for maximum production of leaves for cooking we should be cutting them regularly, we often succumb to the temptation of letting them come into bloom.

WINDOW GARDENS

An old and a young rosemary plant share a windowsill.

A fold-down shelf holds some pots of herbs and a succulent rock garden. Some young sage plants trail from the small hanging pot. The fern is *Polypodium aureum* and the large plant on the left is *Drymonia stenophylla*.

A cow creamer, coffeepot, cup and saucer, and cut crystal sugar bowl planted with herbs make an amusing arrangement.

Herbs Grown Outdoors

Our herb gardens are directly modeled on those of the English. No other nation has retained so much interest in formal plantings as they have. Their climate is much milder in winter than ours and, over the whole southern tier, hard frosts are relatively rare. This has meant that many varieties of plants from southern Europe, especially Italy and Greece, can become tolerant of the climate with selection and breeding. Thus the repertory of the English herb garden is a mixture of hardy plants and ones that are half-tender and may need some protection in winter.

In establishing the English herbal strains in this country, gardeners have had to consider that the winters here are far more severe. And this has eliminated many desirable varieties developed abroad. In other words we are obliged to select winter-hardy plants for outdoor growing. The English have been able to adapt many of our hardy native herbs without much trouble.

Of the English herbs a local nursery lists the following:

Angelica	*Lemon Balm*	*Sorrel (French)*
Bedstraw	*Lovage*	*Southernwood*
Betony	*Mint (several)*	*Sweet Bay (Laurus)*
Bugleweed (Ajuga)	*Nepeta*	*Sweet Cicely*
Catnip	*Onions and Chives*	*Sweet Woodruff*
Chamomile	*Origanum*	*Tansy*
Comfrey	*Orris*	*Tarragon*
Costmary	*Rue*	*Teucrium*
Feverfew	*Sage (two)*	*Thyme (three)*
Horehound	*Salad Burnet*	*Winter Savory*
Hyssop	*Savory*	*Woad*
Lavender (one var.)	*Skirret (Sium)*	*Yarrow*

Myrtle, basil, and rosemary are among those not included, because they are insufficiently winter hardy. The principal native American addition to the herb list has been *Monarda didyma*, Oswego tea, a very handsome subject. Most of the others are poor substitutes for the better culinary herbs, or are grown as herbal medicine curiosities.

Until recently the vast majority of herb nurserymen knew far more about uses, legends, and myths than about horticulture. A visit, to one, with the intention of learning how to grow herbs, was a frustrating experience. The plants chosen for cultivation were usually the most common ones and, in any case, those which were the least trouble in the local soil and climate. Once seeded, chance and Mother Nature were in charge. Plants sold to visitors were badly potted in the worst of soils and little or no attention was given to their good appearance. For the cultist this made for quaintness but for the modern grower it offered very poor ornamental material to grow either in his garden or house. An indoor grower, intimately living with his plants, soon learns more about them than such outdoor gardeners learn in a lifetime.

It should be added that from these herb farms the seeds are of the poorest varieties and often bring into the home their quota of the eggs of aphids, mites, and other insect pests. Getting good clean stock of the finest varieties has been nearly impossible.

Greenhouse-grown Herbs

When plants are grown in a greenhouse the environment is quite different from that of the garden. It is, for one thing, a place for growing and maintaining the plants, not for formal arrangements. But it does offer conditions in which a great many more different kinds of plants can live happily. Here the exceptions are the true winter-hardy plants but they are far outnumbered by the tender ones which are those the indoor gardener prefers.

Greenhouse temperatures can be controlled to agree with three important ranges in winter. One permits near-freezing conditions. A few borderline hardy herbs do best here. Another range is that between 45° and 65° F, which is most suitable for such cool-growing herbs as the geraniums and the half-tender European culinary herbs. The tropical house is kept above 60° F at all times and permits the growing of a vast range of plants, partly standard herbs from southern Europe and the Mediterranean plus many more from the really hot regions of the world —herbaceous plants, shrubs, and small trees.

Protected from drought, damaging wind, snow, and cloudbursts, the plants grow far better than outdoors and develop a more attractive appearance. Plants from a greenhouse, therefore, unless they have been forced unmercifully, are neater, healthier, and more reliable. The indoor grower should buy his plants from greenhouse-grown stock whenever possible. He will have much greater choice of material and superior plants. Furthermore, the very fact that the herbs have been grown indoors ensures that there will be less shock in moving them to your home. Finally, the plants growing in a greenhouse are those chosen for tenderness. They do not require freezing conditions and are therefore the ones you want for the house.

5

Selecting the Right Plants

Why Buy Plants?

Plants should be bought whenever possible in preference to seed. Usually indoors we do not need more than a few plants—so why waste seed and why take even a greater chance on the quality of the plants produced from them? Since we can multiply almost all the herbs vegetatively from cuttings, we can start with one plant of any variety. If it grows well and is satisfactory in other respects, we will, with very little trouble, have all the plants we want and plenty more to give away to friends. A visit to a nursery introduces us to numerous varieties and permits us to pick out a plant that especially appeals to us. It is an altogether more rewarding experience.

In regard to many tropical herbs we are still dependent upon seed, and even that is not easy to come by. As the indoor hobby grows in popularity, no doubt the greenhouses will carry more tropical plants with herbal characteristics. But for the standard and traditional herbs, buy plants.

Field-grown Plants

Field-grown plants are potted up in the same soil in which they have been grown, along with useful worms but also any noxious insects which may be, and usually are, present. Some of these may be harmless enough outside but they surely are a nuisance in the home.

Often the clay pots have no holes in the bottom. In the nursery and old-fashioned greenhouses, the pots are plunged in the soil and, without a hole, need fewer waterings. In the house this preserves the soil moisture a little longer but makes it difficult to sense the dryness of the medium, causing watering to become pretty much of a gamble, with waterlogging the major risk.

Plants that have been sitting in their pots for a long time waiting for someone to adopt them are usually ferociously pot-bound. This keeps them small, which suits the nurseryman, but makes them much more subject to damage from the shock of moving and change in their culture when we buy them.

Choosing the Right Clones

As do all plants, herbs belong to families, genera, and species. We assume that when we buy at a nursery a plant with a certain species name it will be the same one as we would find at any other nursery either here or abroad. But this is not the case and comes about in the following manner.

The principal herbs have been grown, since time immemorial, in many places. When the same species of a plant, native, let us say, to southern Italy, was cultivated for centuries in northern Italy, in France, or in England, changes usually took place in a number of characteristics. Not only soil composition but climate has an effect on the aroma and flavor of herb plants. In addition, the growers in these places might select plants that varied somewhat from the normal or that they thought were superior. In the end, the plant grown in England would be very different indeed from the one growing cultivated or wild in southern Italy. A further change would take place if a plant from Greece and one from Italy were hybridized. The species would remain the same but the resultant plant might bear very little resemblance in respect to its herbal qualities to either of its parents.

Variation takes place whenever seeds are used for propagation, and any number of forms may develop with time. If any one preferred variety is selected, and we want to perpetuate its qualities, we must multiply it by vegetative means—in other words grow more plants from pieces of root, stem, or leaf. The resultant plant is called a clone and any clone may have a set of characteristics that make it better for one purpose or another. It may be better suited to an English than an American climate, or vice versa, to outdoor than indoor growing, have a stronger or weaker flavor, or be much more or less subject to disease. If we compare plants growing in somewhat similar circumstances, such as greenhouses or herb farms, we can often, by observing the vigor and manner of growth, and by tasting and smelling, tell the difference between a superior or an inferior clone for our purposes. Usually the plants at these places *are* clones because any nurseryman who values the quality of his product will grow the more variable plants by vegetative propagation. It won't, for reasons nobody can explain, make any difference with some plant species, and in others it is decisive. Almost always where you see a list of varieties or strains you can be sure that they are variable plants and that you must be selective in acquiring them. For example we recently bought on faith a plant which had all the leaf and growth characteristics of oregano. It turned out to be as tasteless as grass.

Buying Seed

The only advice we can give on seed is to try one seedsman's product, stick with it if satisfied but change if you do not have good results. There is no way of judging seed before buying it.

Change of Environment

Any plant brought from the garden or greenhouse into a home is subjected to a shock which is temporarily damaging. The change is not only one of "climate" but of treatment. The greater the degree of change from the conditions to which the plant has been accustomed or to which it is best adapted, the greater the risk of loss. Survival often depends on taking measures immediately, if possible, to ease the transition. Unfortunately, we must also protect our other plants from contamination by the new one and quarantine it. In doing so, we may have to subject it for a period to further upsets.

Obviously, the knocking about a plant receives when it is transported from one place to another is disturbing. In the process there are also rapid changes in temperature and from close air to sudden drafts. When the plant arrives in its new home, unless it is very tough, it will simply rest up and stop growing for a while. During this first period don't expose it to intense light or extreme temperatures. Put it where it receives some illumination and moderate temperatures. If you can also provide rather high humidity it will help a great deal. Often just enclosing a plant in a plastic bag will revive it. This is a pretty general panacea for plants in shock.

There is not much you can do about other forms of shock. If your herb comes from outdoors it is not going to like the dry and still air or the pollution of a city apartment but it will adapt in time. Greenhouse-grown plants usually have it easier, especially if room humidity can be kept fairly high—at least 40 percent, in the case of tropicals 50 percent. Gentle watering and going easy on fertilizer in the first period also help.

Change to the Indoor Environment

No matter whether you buy a herb plant at an outdoor nursery or a greenhouse, it suffers a traumatic experience in being moved to your home. You know nothing about how it has been treated previously as to all the essentials of culture but you can be sure that your methods will be different. No wonder herbs get rattled in the early stages of your ownership. Suddenly they are placed on different schedules of light, watering, and fertilizing, to say nothing of dozens of other variables involving your personal ways of handling plants. In fact uncertainty regarding the best system to follow in respect to the culture of a particular plant may cause you to vacillate between different ones and to cause further confusion. The marvel is how well most of the plants do stand up under this treatment and that they do gradually adapt to your whims and vagaries.

Location in the house is an important element in judging the suitability of herbs for your home and their potential to adapt to different situations. In the following sections we describe some of the characteristics of typical home conditions.

Sun Porches. These are of two types, heated and unheated. Nowadays most of them are heated. All rooms with ceilings provide less lighting than outdoors—less than half as much even close to the windows. Because of the angle of the sun, the porch receives more hours of direct sunlight in winter than summer. The unheated sun porch rarely if ever goes below freezing and is suitable for tender but not tropical plants. The heated sun porch will be tolerated by tropical *and* tender plants but not those requiring temperatures close to freezing in winter.

Growth continues in winter, as in a greenhouse, but at a slower rate. Excellent humidity can be maintained either by growing a great number of plants or adding humidifying equipment. In the north, bloom can be expected only in summer and close to the window. Rear areas of the room may or may not have good reflected light, depending on the height of the ceiling and the depth of the room. All in all, the environment is easier on plants than outdoor growing and inferior to that of a greenhouse. If artificial supplementary light is added, the room can have all the advantages of interior growing without its disadvantages.

Because of the roominess of a sun porch, it is a particularly good place to experiment with large pots or tubs of some of the tropical bushes and young trees with fragrant flowers or aromatic leaves. Vines can grow around the window area. Small plants, on the other hand, are a bit difficult to display unless a considerable amount of space is devoted to a deep shelf close to the panes. Hanging pots and baskets do particularly well.

Window Growing. Even in the country plants close to a window enjoy less light than on a sun porch. In the city they suffer from a further reduction due to aerial pollution and dirt. Altogether this is, at present, the least satisfactory situation in the house from every standpoint. Even the appearance of the plants is poor as they all tend to grow toward the sun and away from your vision, while the glare from outside causes us to see them merely as silhouettes. Consistent bloom is almost impossible except for a few very easy plants such as African violets and wax begonias. Herbs will bloom only occasionally. Any very attractive arrangement is well nigh impossible.

The principal problem is lack of space. Only plants in the center of the window receive light for a few hours of a sunny day. As you move to the side, the duration of bright daylight is drastically reduced. The southern exposure is often too bright for short periods, and north is only satisfactory for definite shade lovers.

Many of the kits for growing herbs, which have appeared on the market, imply that good results can be achieved in a window. With a very small number of plants it is just possible but in most instances the plants will elongate and become unsightly rather fast. They just won't tolerate, in addition to the shortened sunlight day, periods of cloudy weather. Arranging supplementary light in a window is difficult and even humidifying the environment presents special problems; the window is often set directly over a radiator for instance.

TRAY GARDEN WITH ROCK

A large round copper tray is first covered with a layer of perlite. Japanese pebbles are ready for use.

After the perlite has been spread evenly, the pebbles are distributed over the surface. The soft brush is there to remove dust on the pebbles and the rim of the tray.

A large chunk of Featherrock has been hollowed out by scraping and working with a light hammer and long screwdriver. The herb is an irregularly grown young *Rosmarinus prostratum,* which with care and pruning will stay small.

Pot and all have disappeared inside the rock. Moss has been settled round the top and the plant oriented to the shape of the stone.

The rock and its herb have been set on the tray. With time and training it will become progressively more attractive.

All set to go with the salad. Here we have our own French basil, red wine vinegar, the tomato, and the fresh-cut salad greens.

Herbs are a delightful surprise for the decoration of individual place settings. Any uniform little containers will do for small herbs. Here we have used little metal cups.

Simple place mat setting using cup and small rosemary plant.

6

General Culture of Herbs Indoors

Because there are so many different types of herbs from regions which vary greatly in climate, it is impossible to give a series of cultural directions that will apply generally. By consulting the cultural descriptions in our herb list, pages 81 to 181, you will gain a far better idea of how to deal with them. However, there are certain general rules of indoor growing which you might follow for the major categories.

Temperature. Most of us prefer a home which is warm in winter—65° F or higher, perhaps dropping to 55° at night. This will not do for plants that require a winter freeze. Happily those that do are in large part not particularly attractive for indoor growing. Of the others there are usually varieties that will prefer indoor warmth. Greenhouse-grown plants are usually safe. English varieties of herbs generally do better in the house than American ones, at least those usually grown outdoors.

Among the more important herbs, a major exception is tarragon, which definitely requires some wintering. If you can put your pot outside the window for a period of two weeks of frost, the plant can be brought in again, cut down to the ground, and will sprout from the roots.

The tropical herbs benefit from our warm houses and present no temperature problems.

Light. The general rule is to give the best light you can in the house. However, separate the herbs that really need brilliant illumination from those that are not as demanding. Set the former in the center of the window or the light garden, and place the others on the sides.

Humidity. The standard garden herbs are rather indifferent to humidity. They will grow more luxuriantly if the humidity is higher but will not suffer in a dry house.

Tropical herbs require a humidity above 50 percent in most cases. Obviously desert plants do not. If you have a dry house try aloes, sempervivums and such which will get along fine in the same conditions as the garden herbs.

Watering. In the average home, pots dry out fast and most deaths are due to underwatering. It is true that we can also overwater, but the risk is rather less.

Here are some rules to follow regarding herbs:

1. Except for a few of the tropicals, do not allow the pot to sit in a saucer full of water.

2. Plants are more tolerant of watering during warm spells than cold periods. When the air is cool do not water until the surface of the soil is dry. During hot spells you do not have to wait for surface dryness since the evaporation is more rapid.

3. You will have to water less if you use plastic pots.

4. If your plant is in rapid growth, it will absorb more water. If it stops growing, be very careful that excess moisture in the soil has been absorbed before watering again. A plant that is not growing actively will rot out if its roots are excessively moist. An ailing plant should be kept just moist.

5. Observe your plants. You will notice that some are heavier drinkers than others. Adjust your watering accordingly.

6. The ideal temperature for the water is the same as the air of your room. Do not water with liquid much cooler than air temperature.

7. Pay attention to our notes on the individual herbs. Some like very wet conditions and hardly ever object to wetness. Others prefer a rather dry soil.

Fertilizer. Packaged fertilizers, available at variety stores, many florist shops, garden centers, and elsewhere, are always labeled with their chemical content. The basic chemicals required by plants are nitrogen (nitrates), phosphorus (phosphates), and potassium (potash). On the label they will be given numbers representing the percentages in the mix in this same invariable order. For instance 12–15–9 means 12 percent nitrates, 15 percent phosphates, and 9 percent potash. There are many formulations for different horticultural purposes. But the herb grower will have best results with high nitrate fertilizers. In other words the first number, indicating the nitrogenous content, should be higher than the other two—how much does not make too much difference. Since minute quantities of other elements, listed as "trace elements," are valuable or necessary in plant growth, choose packaged fertilizers which state that they contain them.

Chemical fertilizers are soluble in water and the label states what the manufacturer considers the correct amount to be used with each gallon of water—for instance, one tablespoon.

Organic fertilizers are fish emulsions, seaweed extracts, and so on. The content of chemical nutrients is listed in the same way as for chemical fertilizers, and the dosage is also indicated.

Most indoor growers fertilize in one of two ways. Either they feed with every watering, in which case they should use approximately one-twelfth the dilution indicated on the label—instead of one tablespoon to a gallon of water, use one-twelfth of a tablespoon, which is equivalent to one-quarter teaspoon. Or they fertilize once a week, in which case one-quarter the strength indicated on the label should be used.

Most northern herbs of the shrubby type are accustomed to poor soil and little fertilizer. Tropicals with fleshy stems and large, luxuriant leaves prefer more.

Overfertilizing burns roots. Fertilizer salts gradually build up in the soil of a pot with damaging effect to a plant. Once every couple of months it is therefore advisable to run clear water through the soil of your pots for a few moments to leach out the impurities.

Pests and Pesticides. Plants attract insects indoors as well as in the garden. Almost inevitably, therefore, your herb plants will be infested at some time or other. We don't like using any of the insecticides and consider them absolutely taboo on plants that will be used in cooking. In the house the area of infestation is not large and it is altogether possible, with a little patience and effort, to get rid of pests without using a pesticide. With plants that are not used in any way for food one of the less dangerous pesticides may be considered in an extreme case of infestation. Above all, avoid systemic pesticides with all the food plants.

The principal pests are:

Mealybug—white fuzzy creatures which are visible.

Scale—tiny oval brown mounded shells adhering to branches and the veins of leaves.

Both of these can be eliminated by careful washing of the stems and leaves in lukewarm soap and water. Visible insects are surrounded at maturity by their offspring which are invisible. So the washing must be thorough and be repeated every few days for at least two weeks. With a brush and rubbing alcohol you can also swab off the insects and proceed with a thorough brushing of all the surfaces of the plant.

Mites—numerous tiny crablike creatures which are invisible. Anytime that leaves turn yellow and drop off under normal culture, suspect mites. They can be seen with a ten power magnifying glass (available in hobby shops). If you can't see any moving insects look for fine white threads and egg cases on the undersides of leaves.

Wash the plant thoroughly in soapy water with one tablespoon of chlorine to the gallon. Work a fine paintbrush into the axils of the leaves and over all the undersurfaces. Mites hate water, and several subsequent washings ought to finish them off.

Lethal pesticides for the above insects but risky also for humans are Malathion for mealybug and scale, and Kelthane for mites. Use rubber gloves and a mask when handling these chemicals.

White Fly. These are tiny white flies that hop out from under leaves and flutter for short distances. Their eggs may completely cover the undersurface of a leaf and, since their cycle is two to three days, multiplication is overwhelming if not stopped. In the greenhouse they are a great nuisance but indoors we can cope with them. Just wash off the plant with lukewarm soapy water rubbing the bottoms of the leaves thoroughly with your fingers. Repeat every couple of days for four to six washings.

Aphids. Quite good-sized green insects that cluster on the stems of plants. They can be washed off rather easily with soap and water.

Nematodes. These are of two kinds, leaf and root. They are tiny worms which are invisible in the soil and visible with a strong magnifying glass on the edges of leaves where they display an amount of activity which is terrifying. A sick-looking plant that has small nodules on the roots is infected. Don't pay any attention to big nodules because these are usually regular water storage or nitrogen fixation nodules. Whenever you see the leaf kind or find the nodules, throw out the plant and its pot—fast. Infestation of your other plants may follow any delay. There are cures but they involve the use of very poisonous insecticides.

For small soil creatures, little black and white bugs, a drench of one tablespoon of chlorine to a gallon of water will usually get rid of them.

None of these insects are dangerous to humans or likely to get on your food or clothing. They feed only on plants. So don't get into a panic because you find them. Go to work and save the plant.

A HERB GARDEN CENTERPIECE

This Rubbermaid turntable is provided with clear plastic wedge-shaped containers with covers. It is used for storing beans, rice, and other dry products and doubles as a server for party niblets and salads. A third use can be as an ornamental planting for herbs. Make it your dining table centerpiece. The first step is to fill it partway with perlite. Measure the depth of your first pot.

The pot is buried. Now have a go at other herbs in small pots.

You can work with each wedge separately, as the whole arrangement comes apart.

Here we are with the finished piece.

Another arrangement utilizing a scented geranium, pineapple sage, *Lavandula dentata*, and the curry plant *(Helichrysum angustifolium)*. What an aromatic setting for a gourmet dinner.

7

Herb Gardens in Terrariums

A number of herbs are adapted to terrarium culture which is so popular at present. In fact the old-fashioned woodland plant terrarium has a repertory largely made up of herbs and, though growers probably never thought of them this way, there is no reason why we should not include these plants and the method in a book for herb gardeners. As we learn more about the tropical herbs we have no doubt that many terrarium arrangements will employ the smaller types.

Terrariums are plastic or glass containers that are kept closed most of the time to preserve the humidity within. Because moisture and air recirculate inside, the plants do not need ventilation. However, the modern terrarium is kept open partway during days of extreme heat— over 80°. The principal problem with such closed containers is maintaining the correct amount of moisture. If this is done right the first time, very little attention will be needed thereafter.

The majority of people tend to overwater their terrariums, which almost invariably leads to disaster. The proper condition is one of just moistness without sogginess or any standing water. If moss is used it should lie on a bed of gravel with just enough water to make a thin film at the base. Soil should be even drier and needs no drainage. If the soil when squeezed feels just moist and does not clump but remains loose under the pressure, that would be just right. If it clumps, it is too wet. Do not fear that a dryish state of this kind is too dry. The plants will flourish when the soil is in this condition.

Our chief innovation in terrarium planting is the use of pots instead of the old custom of setting plants directly into the soil. This is only not advisable with two specialized groups of plants. The carnivorous plants require sphagnum moss and the woodland plants regular acid soil or acid woods moss and must be allowed their freedom in tank or bowl. Planting pots in terrariums is particularly adapted to tropical blooming and foliage plants. No doubt in the future our indoor herb gardens will include more of these than formerly.

Terrariums come in many shapes and sizes. We prefer above all others the rectangular fish tank of glass, for it displays the plants themselves far better than other forms. Round bowls are next in adaptability. We prefer glass to plastic because it remains clean while the latter clouds up and stays fogged longer. Due to acid action and the grittiness of the soil, plastic usually deteriorates rapidly and becomes progressively less transparent and attractive.

A tank serves as an excellent display case where your plants need a minimum of attention. Many of the small herbs can be planted in ornamental small pots and placed inside a tank whose bottom has been covered with a layer of Japanese or other decorative pebbles. Don't crowd the pots but rather strive for a pleasing arrangement.

Never place terrariums in direct sunlight, which will simply cook them, unless you remove the cover completely, whereupon they are no longer terrariums and require normal watering and care. With reflected light this is unnecessary.

On the other hand do not expect a terrarium to flourish in the middle of a living room. Adequate light must be provided. The ideal fixture is a 24-inch fixture with two 20-watt fluorescent tubes. For round terrariums you may use a Circline lamp. Keep the lights on for fourteen hours each day. With artificial lighting the terrarium can be placed on a table in any dark corner, in a bookshelf or room divider or even in an unused fireplace. For culinary herbs a spot on the back of the kitchen worktable is both decorative and useful.

The Carnivorous Terrarium

In our list sundews and pitcher plants do best in a terrarium, and believe it or not, they are rated as herbs. They can be arranged and planted in a moment. The best medium is sphagnum moss. This can be bought in bags as dried whole sphagnum or collected alive from a neighboring bog. Do not use milled dried sphagnum. Fill the terrarium, preferably a tank, with four or five inches of well-packed sphagnum thoroughly moistened. Set the plant into the medium, cover, place under light, and the arrangement will need no care as long as you do not encounter high temperatures.

Other plants you can grow along with your medicinal carnivores are pinguicula (butterwort, a perfectly good herb too) and Venus flytrap.

The Woodland Herb Terrarium

We list bearberry, wintergreen, partridgeberry, and pipsissewa. This combination has been popular for ages in the windows of farmhouses. Recently, in the desire to conserve the wild plants these terrariums have been frowned upon but one can still get the plants from wild flower nurseries. (Do not dig them up yourself in the woods.) The dark greenery and red berries are very Christmasy. Plant in any kind of glass or plastic container in any kind of moss, preferably live. If you use soil, Rich Mix will be adequate. These plants need very little light and can be placed at the side of your light garden or a window. They do, however, prefer cool temperatures, below 80° and down to 45°. Vinca and small thymes will do well with these plants along with miniature ferns.

We start our terrarium with perlite, Lean Mix, and rocks. The rocks are actually puffed up slag from an old limekiln and the flowing types are from the same source but heavier. Japanese pebbles are used for base decoration and moss as a filler on top of pots.

The plants we'll use. The four tall plants are lemon basil, basil, artemisia, and rosemary. In the second row are pineapple sage, rosemary, dittany, and marjoram. In the front row are lemon verbena, lavender dentata, and lemon thyme.

We have started building, using as our container a 20-gallon tropical fish tank. Perlite is laid down as a base and Lean Mix built up over it. Then rocks are arranged and an artemisia and a dittany plant are already in place.

The right side of the terrarium. Plants have been added and pebbles have been laid over the perlite to simulate a shore.

The finished terrarium.

Detail of the right side.

Left side of the terrarium.

Close-up of the left side of the terrarium.

Herb terrarium. The plants in their pots are simply set on a surface of perlite covered with Japanese pebbles. The terrarium will be covered with a pane of glass or a sheet of clear plastic.

Small bog terrarium. Sundews, butterworts, pitcher plant, Venus-flytrap, ferns—all planted in sphagnum moss.

8

Fluorescent Light Culture

Herbs under Artificial Light

Nothing has helped the popularity of herb growing indoors so much as the discovery that we can grow them under artificial light. By using it, we are freed from a great many handicaps associated with both porch and window gardening. The seeds in the kits will really flourish anywhere in the house with its assistance. The whole problem of staging plants properly for room decoration can now be solved. Light is available every day, all day, to the plants, and they respond by growing symmetrically and producing bloom.

No longer do winter and summer make much difference. Indoor temperatures encourage growth at all times and the light is the same. Plants can be manipulated and arranged much more easily to receive the right amount of light for their needs. If humidifying equipment is added, the level can easily be maintained at 50 percent. For these and other reasons some plants react better in the light garden than in a greenhouse and will grow more continuously and bloom more often.

A particular advantage is in the matter of space. No apartment is too small to find room for a few plants and a light unit. The fixtures can be hung in bathrooms (in a cabinet under the washbowl), under cabinets or tables in the kitchen, in shelving, under tables. Cellars offer plenty of room for larger installations. A corner or a section along the wall of a living room on the floor can be turned into a garden by attaching the fixtures to the wall above it.

There will be no glare if valances or curved reflectors are provided. Even big plants can be lighted by modern floods.

Plants which were formerly considered only for greenhouse conditions can now grow in your living room or kitchen. Although we list only

Here a small herb garden is lighted by two twenty-watt twenty-four-inch fluorescent lamps with reflector. The fixture is suspended from the bottom of the kitchen cabinet by S hooks hung from cup hooks. No attempt is made here for elegance, and we are too busy trying out different herbs and growing them for cuttings to give the necessary care. But such an installation can also be a showpiece with carefully trained plants.

We had to improvise a light garden for our herbs at the end of our pantry because of a sudden influx of plants. This is a 48-inch fixture with two tubes and reflector. We suspended it by means of flexible wire temporarily so that height could be adjusted quickly. The whole installation took only a few minutes.

a few of these, there are great numbers of tropical plants with aromatic leaves or fragrant flowers that will grow small enough or can be trimmed to remain that way under the lights. Half the fun of the new herb gardening indoors is experimenting with plants that have not been possible in outdoor herb gardens.

Fluorescent fixtures are inexpensive and available everywhere. If you live in an apartment in or out of the city, this is the best way to grow your herbs.

We can give here only a short summary of information on the use of artificial light in growing herbs. Much of the detail will be found in *The Indoor Light Gardening Book* (Crown).

The advantages offered the indoor herb grower by fluorescent light are impressive. They mean that you are no longer dependent on daylight and this, especially in the cities, often makes the difference between whether you can or cannot grow vigorous herb plants in the house. The fact that the lights are on every day, all day, produces much more regular growth and saves your plants from those long periods of cloudy days which are so common in winter. And this points up the advantage it offers in winter growing, which is exactly the time of year when we need it most. In summer we are often away from home, often do less cooking, and are not nearly so dependent on greenery, bloom, or fragrance. In winter we have had to do without virtually all of this in the past unless we had a particularly well-lighted sun porch. Now all seasons are much the same anywhere in the house and our herb garden indoors is at its height just when we need it and can enjoy it most.

Essentially a minimal light garden consists of a two-tube fluorescent fixture set beneath a cabinet or shelf, with the plants growing in their pots set in saucers or trays below. The standard lengths and wattages for the beginning growers are 20-watt, 24-inch and 40-watt, 48-inch tubes. Later on you may install the longer and more effective 8-foot lamps. The fixtures are just slightly longer than the lamps. They are attached to any surface by means of screws or hung from it by means of hooks and chains. If you install more tubes side by side in a wider garden area you gain not only in space but in amount of illumination. A 6-inch distance between the tubes is the maximum advisable. Increasing the number of tubes and setting them three inches apart increases the intensity of the light and improves growth.

The lights are left on for fourteen to sixteen hours each day and turned on and off by an automatic timer. Distance from the lamps varies according to the plant. Seedlings and cuttings should be within an inch or two. The tops of sun-loving plants also have to be nearly as close, while plants which are described as shade-loving may be set with their tops as much as 12 inches below the lamps. The center of the tubes is the brightest area and there is some falloff at the sides.

The experienced light gardener uses ordinary commercial tubes available everywhere, which are the least expensive and probably as effective as any fluorescent source of light. Lamps labeled as "growth" tubes are not necessarily more effective and are much more expensive. The lamps used are Cool White and Warm White which are made by all manufacturers.* We use them alternately in our fixtures. In a two-tube fixture there will be one of each; in a four-tube fixture there will be two of each in alternation (a, b, a, b). Tubes should be replaced after a year of use.

In this book all our directions for the use of herbs under fluorescent light are calculated for a 2-tube 24-inch fixture. With larger installations you can do better than we have indicated.

Those who are concerned about an energy crisis should take courage regarding fluorescent light from the fact that it uses less than a third of the energy required by the same amount of light from an incandescent lamp. Even the larger double-tube fixture, under which you can grow quite a herb garden, uses only 80 watts, or the equivalent of an incandescent reading lamp for one person.

The disadvantage for the light gardener with a small installation is that he must grow plants that are not more than 18 inches in height.

*Lately we have used TruBloom lamps by Verilux, Inc.

However, we are learning that even large trees and shrubs, as young plants, can be dwarfed by trimming and maintained that way for years. The art started with northern trees but tropical material is proving equally amenable. Also an 18-inch plant in the house can be quite impressive. Larger plants can be grown under fluorescent light but require extensive installations. Spot and flood incandescent lamps are not sufficiently effective and too hot even for large foliage plants unless provided with a dichroic filter like General Electric's Cool Beam. However, those who wish to go to the considerable expense can grow any size plant with a combination of Lucalox and Multi-Vapor lamps.

Tiered stands and carts with fluorescent lights are manufactured by a number of companies and, though not attractive furniture for a living room, do an effective job of growing. You are far better off to build your own with shelving, or under overhead cabinets.

Step-by-Step Care of a Herb Indoors

Quarantining

Any field-grown or greenhouse plant may harbor insects. Those at garden centers and florist shops often pick them up while waiting to be sold. No place is free of them for long. Thus, the first step in introducing a plant into your home is to quarantine it for at least two weeks. As it needs a rest anyway this can only do it good. If you don't religiously follow this rule you will, sooner or later, start an epidemic among any other plants you possess. Keep it in a place with reflected light and away from drafts. Water very sparingly until you see signs of active growth. Do not fertilize at all.

If insects turn up on the stems and leaves during the period, follow the suggestions on page 39. Provided it is a plant that will never be used with food take pot and all and enclose it in a clear plastic bag along with a small piece of No-Pest Strip for eight hours and follow this with a watering that includes a soil insecticide. This will probably solve the problem.

If after this period the plant is clean, you can introduce it to your other plants.

A special problem arises when plants are grown in the house from seed. Very often they develop insect infestations when they are a couple of inches high due to eggs brought in with the seeds themselves. In that case, remove all the seedlings to quarantine for two weeks and wash them thoroughly every two days in lukewarm water with one tablespoon of Clorox to a gallon.

Repotting

For our demonstration we have chosen a pot of *Rosmarinus officinalis,* or rosemary. This is a good example of a nursery-grown plant and

Rosemarinus officinalis—rosemary. The plant is already very large for the small clay pot.

was chosen for its generally healthy appearance and for its single stem, which permitted us to photograph it more easily. The plant has passed through quarantine and is ready to pursue its new career indoors. It is the most vigorous and rapid-growing type, best for cutting. Bonsai hobbyists find rosemary a perfect plant but prefer the slower growing *R. prostratus.* Note the tall growth, the development of branches near the bottom, and the rather stiff silvery leaves.

Officinalis is a species name that turns up constantly with the traditional herbs. It meant originally (according to Stearn, *Botanical Latin,* Thomas Nelson, London) a shop, later a monastic storeroom, then a herb store, pharmacy, or drug shop. Today it means a medicinal plant. In the past a medicinal use was always rated more important than a culinary one, even for so important a flavoring herb as rosemary.

The pot is of clay and 3 inches in diameter at the top. On the bottom there is a round thin spot that has not been broken. The nurseryman prefers it this way because the roots cannot work their way through the bottom into the soil. If it were to do this, and the plant was unsold for a long period, a considerable root system could develop outside the pot. When he came to digging up the pot the nurseryman would find that he had to damage this root to break the pot free from the soil. The closed bottom also helps the pot retain moisture.

If we want to remove the plant from this pot, the closing at the bottom makes it much more difficult because of the vacuum it creates. The same problem arises with the tin cans in which larger plants are

The bottom of the pot, showing the closed hole.

Using a screwdriver to break the hole in the bottom of the pot.

often shipped from southern points. Our first step, then, is to break through the bottom of our container. As soon as we have the plant in the house the hole should be opened with the jab of a screwdriver against the surface. The tool will break right through and, with a couple of twists, the hole will be completely round. Have no fear of breaking the rest of the pot—the covering of the hole is very thin.

Decanting the Plant

Before knocking a plant out of its pot, we should make sure that it has been well watered so that the soil will stick together. If you try to remove a plant from a dry pot you will find that the soil breaks away gradually, leaving the roots bare. Our object is to have the whole contents of the pot slip out in one piece without damage to the roots. Allow the water to drain for at least a half hour before decanting.

Rap the rim of the pot smartly on the side of a table or any other hard surface. Use one hand to hold the pot and one to fit under the plant and support the soil. With a couple of bangs the plant and its soil will break free, be caught in the other hand, and be quite undamaged. The soil is compacted to such a degree that you are able to handle the ball rather freely without disturbing it.

Rapping the rim of the pot on the edge of a table to break the soil ball and plant free.

Pot Binding

Sometimes a plant from a nursery has very little root. A cutting has been rooted under ideal conditions from an actively growing part of the plant but has not spread far at the time you acquire it. These plants should be left in their pots until they have grown more root and foliage. If they start to wilt they should be enclosed in a plastic bag for a few days. This may save them.

Our plant, on the other hand, is pot-bound. This is a condition which arises when it has been grown for too long a time in too small a pot. Roots work back and forth in the pot seeking room and forming a solid network. With severe pot binding the plant becomes strangled and any shock, such as moving it to a new home, can damage it severely. Also, since the roots have so little room they need more fertilizer to support the aboveground growth. If you acquire such a plant, it is usually necessary to cut off part of its length immediately so that the roots will be more in proportion to the plant. In most cases we do both —repot the plant and cut it down to a proper size. This will ensure sturdy growth.

We have seen much worse cases of pot binding than our rosemary. Nevertheless the pattern of root is very clear, and it is obvious that the amount of space is inadequate for the roots and for the support of so large a plant.

The plant needs repotting in order to make room for its roots. However, because we are going to grow it indoors, this is not that simple. First of all, its soil is inferior. In the greenhouse it is quite adequate because of high humidity and the desire of the nurseryman to slow up growth. But indoors we want this type of plant to grow faster so that we can cut leaves for our herb cabinet and multiply the plant for friends . . . or shape it into a decorative specimen. Also a larger pot will look in better proportion. So we need new soil and a new pot. And the pot should be of plastic, which retains moisture far better indoors.

Potting can take place during or immediately after the quarantine period as long as the plant appears to be in good condition.

In order to keep the process of propagation separate from potting and culture we show how we take a cutting of this rosemary plant on pages 64–73.

A relatively mild example of pot binding. Notice the network of roots. Often the roots form a solid coil at the bottom of the pot and a solid net along the sides so that it is very difficult for them to break free even if given more room to spread.

Cleaning the Roots

Removing the old soil involves washing away all but a small residue. But before we do this we should warn you that it should never be done to plants with taproots. A typical taproot plant is the carrot. The root consists of a single underground growth which may be thick or thin and which puts out short side roots. Most of them require, for this reason, very deep pots and resent disturbance. If the plant is in too small a pot, knock it out very gently, being careful to keep the root ball intact and place it in a larger, deeper pot, surrounded by new soil. All members of the carrot family, such as chervil and parsley, are difficult to transplant.

Although cleaning off the roots seems a drastic measure and will stop the growth of the plant for a little while, it will benefit it beyond measure in the long run. If you want to have a perennial plant for a long time it should have good soil and enough space to grow. And it should always be remembered that the bigger the plant is above soil level, the more root it needs below in order to supply sufficient nourishment. Removing the old soil also ensures that any insect eggs which may still be present will be thrown out with the rest.

Fill a pail or basin with lukewarm water and dip the root ball in it. Then shake the plant up and down gently but firmly until all the soil is removed. If it is stubborn, take a one-inch paintbrush and brush around and between the roots. Potting should take place immediately, before the roots dry out.

The rosemary will now go into a slightly larger, 3½-inch, plastic pot. Although the diameter of the top allows for little increase, the shape is broader at the bottom where the roots need the room. There is no advantage in overpotting—quite the contrary. We want to save space for as many plants as possible, for one thing. Also some plants object to having too much room. The next size is usually the right one.

We also illustrate three other sizes—the 2-inch square for good-sized seedlings, the 2½-inch round which is ample for many of the smaller herbs, and the 4-inch square which is close to as large a pot as we would want to use in the indoor herb garden except for old or specimen plants. Old rosemary plants sometimes end up in tubs but, by that time, they have outgrown most light gardens and are difficult to keep in best condition in a window. However, they are beautiful then, and worth the extra effort.

Dunking the soil ball to clean the roots. The place to hold the plant is right at the base of the stem where it is strongest. Don't dangle it from a branch.

Plastic Pots. *Left to right,* 4 inch, 3½ inch, 2 inch, and 2½ inch diameter.

Indoor Potting Soil

The modern indoor grower doesn't use garden soil because (1) it is likely to contain insects, (2) dries out too rapidly for many of our plants, (3) is not sufficiently aerated. The soil can be sterilized in an oven but this is a messy business and not something for most houses and apartments. In the house there is less moving air and the garden soil is too densely packed and fine grained. Packaged houseplant soil consisting of humus, sand, and so on is usually very poor stuff, not as good as a garden loam.

For the house, so-called soilless mix has been found most efficient. It is easy to make your own from ingredients that come packaged and are sold in variety stores, garden centers, and at florist shops. Prepared soilless mixes are also available. We have tried them all and find them inferior to those we make ourselves. The reason is that these mixes are extremely fine textured and use low grades of vermiculite, the smallest size of perlite, and contain large lumps of unshredded peat. We find they tend to clog the roots.

Soilless mix, homemade, is light, gritty, well aerated, and holds water. It can be compounded specially for any need. Above all it just seems to suit the plants. They are much less subject to problems of all kinds in this mix.

So, now we have to make our potting soil.

Components of a Soilless Mix

Peat Moss is partially decayed sphagnum moss which grows in great quantities in the bogs of the United States and Canada. It is fibrous and brown in color. Most American moss is Michigan peat which is inferior in quality. The Canadian moss is finer and performs better. The function of peat moss is to supply the organic fibrous quality to the soil and to hold water, which it does extremely well.

Perlite is a white, granular, gritty material derived from obsidian by subjecting it to extreme heat. It takes the place of sand in the mix. Being extremely light in weight, it easily rises to the top of a pot if the granules are too large. Some growers recommend very coarse perlite but we think that the normal medium grade, most common in the stores, is the best.

Vermiculite. This is mica that has been exfoliated by heat treatment. It is very light in weight and its myriad of crystal platelets gather water by surface tension. In nature the thin slivers are packed together solidly. The heat makes them expand and they form accordionlike cubes, silvery in color. That is what to look for. Do not use large-size building-grade vermiculite, which is also often used as a bed for the barbecue pan. It is not exfoliated properly and the texture is mushy and greasy. This is poison for the plants. Buy bags labeled horticultural grade but even then make sure that it consists of clearly defined cubes.

These materials come in various size packages to meet any need. They are easily stored, and you make just enough mix at any time for the immediate occasion.

Recently perlite has been more difficult to come by because the process of manufacture has produced aerial pollution. If necessary you may substitute hard-fired-clay kitty litter (for instance, Hartz Mountain) in the same proportion. Do not use kitty litter containing a deodorant.

Lime. A controlling factor in the growth of plants is the acidity or alkalinity of the soil. Peat moss is quite acid and becomes progressively more so as we soak it with fertilizer and water. There are some high acid plants—we call them acid lovers—which we will specify in our cultural list. But the majority of herbs prefer a rather neutral condition. For this reason we add lime to our mix whenever the plant we are potting up is not acid loving. If you live in an area with "hard" water this will be unnecessary and countermeasures may have to be taken.

The lime is available as limestone chips, eggshell spun in the blender, or horticultural powdered lime. The easiest way is just to accumulate your breakfast eggshells and grind up a quantity from time to time. Shells should be well dried but need no special cleaning.

Providing sufficient acidity for acid-loving plants presents no special problem. The natural tendency of the peat moss to acidify is aided by the use of high nitrate fertilizers.

Components of the Mix. *Clockwise from left*—perlite, vermiculite, and peat moss. Lime in the middle.

Indoor Herb Soilless Mixes

A great advantage of the soilless mixes is that we can change the formula and need only add more or less of one or the other component. The mixing process is very simple. The dry materials are measured out and placed in a bowl together. Lukewarm water is then added while stirring with a spoon. A "just moist" condition is best. Don't make a mush of your mix.

Three different, very simple, formulas will take care of all your needs. As most of the herbs, of the north at least, are plants of open sunny locations with sterile, leached-out soils, a very lean formula is good for many of them.

Lean Mix

1 part sphagnum peat moss

1 part vermiculite

1 part perlite.

If you use a kitchen measuring cup that means just one cupful of each.

For tropical plants and those requiring a richer soil the following mix is best.

Rich Mix

3 parts sphagnum peat moss

2 parts vermiculite

1 part perlite.

This is the equivalent of three cupfuls of sphagnum peat moss, two of vermiculite, and one of perlite.

For succulent plants—herbs that grow in near desert conditions, such as aloes, sempervivums, and euphorbias—use a Succulent Mix.

Succulent Mix

1 part sphagnum peat moss

2 parts perlite

2 parts vermiculite.

In other words, one cupful of sphagnum peat moss to two each of perlite and vermiculite.

For herbs that are not acid loving, add the following quantities of lime to each quart (four cups) of mix.

Lean Mix—3½ level tablespoons.

Rich Mix—5 level tablespoons.

Succulent Mix—2 tablespoons.

It is better to add the lime before adding water.

Pouring lukewarm water into the Mix.

Stirring the moist Mix.

Potting

All the methods we are showing are really very simple—much more so than the old-fashioned way which involved the use of manures, composts, and special organic soils. If we go into a great deal of detail, it is only for the purpose of taking care of any questions which may stump you because of special circumstances.

Our bare-rooted original rosemary plant is now ready for potting. We have our mix at hand, our pot, and a potting stick to help us pack the pot correctly.

The Potting Stick

Soilless mix has a way of sifting down in the pot unless it is compacted fairly well. We don't want a jammed pot but we don't want air holes either. You will notice the outcurve of the rim of a plastic pot. When we pack soil in from above, some of it can be caught on the inward curve inside the pot and, supported by pressure from the central area, not go downward as it should. This can leave a space between the wall of the pot and the soil. The plant does not mind that but water poured on the surface often just sluices down the inner walls without moistening the soil at the center. We found out by bitter experience that we could give a plant frequent waterings and discover that it was dying of thirst.

It was then that we borrowed an idea from orchid growers who have problems packing their special materials tightly around the roots of their plants without damaging them.

A potting stick is a blunt-pointed dowel which is also a bit broad at the tip. A piece of old broom handle dull-sharpened will do, and in a pinch one can use the handle of a miniature, indoor gardening shovel which has a long, rounded wooden handle.

The bowl full of soilless Mix, the pot, the potting stick, and the rosemary plant. The handle of a meat tenderizing hammer came out, so we shaved the tip to a near point and turned it into a potting stick.

Method of Potting Bare Root

The base of the stalk is held at a level with the rim of the pot with one hand while, with the other, soil is dribbled in and around the roots. As soon as the soil supports the plant, let it go. There will be a tendency for it to sink slightly below the rim where it should be. We don't set it deep because we want to save as much room for the roots as possible.

Now take the potting stick and, while adding more soil, drive it in along the sides of the pot tamping the soil down and, with pressure against the sides, pressing it inward toward the center. Fill up gradually and carefully until the soil is firm all around.

By this means we have avoided damaging pressure from above on the plant and roots while ensuring proper packing of the pot.

Holding the plant and dribbling soil into the pot.

Using the potting stick. Drive it down the wall of the pot and then lever inward to compact the soil in the center. Then add more soil to fill the outside spaces.

Once the potting stick has done its work filling the pot completely with soilless mix, we can press the plant lightly but firmly on both sides so that it is vertical and the soil around the stem well packed.

A Place in the Herb Garden

It remains only to water the newly potted rosemary lightly and find a place in the house where it will be happy.

In the window we are setting it on one side where it will receive partial sun, which is all it needs. Give it a saucer of course to prevent drip.

On a fluorescent-lighted shelf in the living room it can also stand simply in a saucer or be part of a grouping in a tray. Trays come in various shapes, sizes, and materials and which you use is a matter of taste. However, we also want to show one way of providing somewhat more humidity. And that is by filling the bottom of the tray with plastic egg crate cut to size and placing our pots directly on it. When water is poured into the tray within about a quarter of an inch of the top of the crate, it will evaporate around the plants.

Plastic crate is a louver, or light diffuser, often used in the ceilings of elevators. You can buy it from plastics distributors and commercial lighting fixture stores. It comes in sheets two feet wide and four feet long. But you can also sometimes buy a collection of leftover sections much cheaper.

The advantage of plastic crate is that it is very clean and light. The old-fashioned method of using pebbles is much less satisfactory. The tray becomes excessively heavy and the pebbles are harder to keep clean. Aesthetically, the crate looks better in the house.

Potting with the Whole Earth Ball

If your plant is of the kind we have described, which should not have its soil ball disturbed, simply knock it out of its pot, put enough soilless mix in the bottom of the new pot so that the plant will stand nearly even with the rim of the pot, and fill in around it, using your potting stick to tamp down the soil between the sides and the original soil ball.

Multiplying Your Plants

Among the greatest pleasures of indoor gardening with herbs is the experience of multiplying them in order always to have reserve plants of favorites and as gifts for friends. Whereas the usual florist gift plants last only a few weeks, a herb can be a delight for a lifetime.

The best way of propagating indoors is by means of stems or leaves of the plants. In our outdoor gardens we are accustomed to planting seeds almost exclusively. The commercial greenhouses do a great deal of vegetative propagation of perennials to ensure that all the plants have the same qualities. Seed is quite unreliable in this respect. They do grow annuals from seed and almost never multiply them by means of cuttings. We have found that our indoor conditions permit us to propagate many annuals in this way.

Since plants that are brought from the outdoors or the nursery into a strange environment suffer such severe shock, we also want to make sure that we do not lose a plant entirely. Rooting a cutting almost certainly guarantees that this will not happen. And it is a common experience that the plant grown from a cutting, having been grown entirely in our home, does far better than its parent.

Removing top growth from a pot-bound plant or one which has been repotted reduces the strain on the root system. Most branches can be used for propagation.

Propagation of herbs in this way is particularly appropriate because we normally cut off pieces of stem and branch at regular intervals and, since the crop of leaves is often so small as to be worthless in practice, the pieces can be put to work producing new plants for us.

The new horticulture, our evenly heated homes, and artificial light gardening have greatly simplified methods of propagation so that it is easily carried on with very little experience.

You will have noticed that, after our photo of the whole rosemary plant, it became about half as high. This was not due to a bad case of brown thumb but because we removed a section of the plant in order to multiply it. Now we will retrace our steps and show how we "took" the cuttings (in quarantine or during repotting proceedings), planted them, rooted them, and finally potted them up.

Most green-stemmed and shrubby herbs can be propagated by rooting pieces of branch with some leaves attached. As we have already remarked, the method is very simple. But, so that you will have no question unanswered, we will try to fill in the details very carefully.

The Propagation Box

For indoor propagation the best container is one of plastic with a transparent cover. The depth of the container including the cover should be a minimum of 2½ inches.

For most of our cuttings we use plastic bread boxes that are 12 inches long by 5 inches wide and high. The domed top makes it somewhat higher than other containers of comparable length and width. For instance, many large plastic storage boxes have flat tops, a half to a full inch lower. The bread box is of a size that fits well on a shelf at the window or across the shelf under lights. We use it when we want to root at least twenty cuttings, but it will hold a great many more.

Smaller boxes are useful when you want to root only a few cuttings. For instance, a very convenient size is just 5 inches long by 3¼ inches wide by 2½ inches high. For one to five cuttings, depending on size, two plastic old-fashioned glasses set on top of each other, with their open ends together, will do the trick. There is plenty of room for improvisation. The main thing is to remember that the cover must be transparent and that it should fit fairly tight.

The Medium

The "soil" for the cuttings is that same vermiculite that we use in our soilless mix and which is described on page oo. Fill the bottom of your propagation box with at least 1½ inches of dry vermiculite. There should be no holes in the bottom of the box.

The right amount of moisture is the only ticklish part of the whole operation. Remember, once we have added water we will not do it again. If the vermiculite is too wet the cuttings may rot. We have no experience of anyone making it too dry, though it is, of course, possible.

To the vermiculite in small boxes, less than the size of a bread box, add lukewarm water and mix at the rate of one tablespoon at a time.

To the larger boxes start with ½ cup of water and continue a tablespoon at a time until the moment you can feel the moisture—then stop. We, ourselves, have found that ½ cup of water to 4 cups of vermiculite is about right. Remember—the medium should be just barely moist.

If, by chance, you have added too much water, take part of the vermiculite out of the box and add dry vermiculite until the "just barely moist" point is reached.

Your propagation box is now ready. Cover it until the moment you start planting your cuttings.

Where to Cut

Cuttings are taken from the tips of growing stems or branches. You will notice that the leaves are arranged either in pairs opposite each other, or alternately along the stem. Sometimes, as with certain varieties of rosemary, there will be one or more tiny leaves at the base of the big leaf. The place where the leaf joins the stalk is called a leaf node, and the angle between the leaf and the stalk is called the axil. The leaf node is where roots often start or they may come from the bare stalk itself. New top growth grows from a visible or invisible "bud" in the leaf axil.

As far as you are concerned, the only problem is how far along the stem you should cut. The rule for most plants is not less than three nodes from the tip or 1½ inches. If the leaves are crowded on the stem you will have to use the measurement. If the distance between the leaf nodes is greater, you should count.

Even when the leaf nodes are farther apart, cuttings can be made which are more than 1½ inches long. In fact they may run up to three or four. But, remember, the longer the cutting the fewer you can take from a plant. And there is one other point to consider. If there is too much leafy growth on the cutting, the energy will all go into maintaining the leaves and not into making roots. One reason why we don't want our medium to be too wet is that if the plant is satisfied with the water it is receiving it will not make the effort of rooting. The near dry medium forces it to put out roots in order to survive.

Cuttings should also be from young, green shoots, not from older wood. The latter may put out roots but it is a longer process and more uncertain.

We have to count nodes only when they are far apart. Our rosemary has them packed so densely that we cannot count them. But an inch and a half of the tip will have all the leaf buds we need for branching.

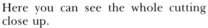

Here you can see the whole cutting close up.

Taking a second cutting from the rosemary plant. Such drastic trimming does the plant no harm. On the contrary it will now begin to branch actively. Be careful that you plant the cutting with the top up and the bottom in the soil.

The first and second cutting. The plant now can bush out. The pot stands on a square of plastic egg crate.

How to Cut

The older books all required us to use special horticultural knives made for the purpose of taking cuttings. This is no longer necessary in the house. We are dealing with soft, small cuttings and a pair of small, sharp scissors will do. For most work nail scissors are fine. Don't worry about sterilizing or even excessive cleanliness. Contamination is most unusual indoors. Just be sure to make a clean, smooth cut.

Hormone Powder

Compelling scientific explanations have been given for the advantages of using hormone powder to encourage root development in cuttings. In practice many indoor gardeners have given up its use, finding that they have no trouble rooting cuttings without it. Undoubtedly the efficiency of the propagation box indoors is greater than can be provided for masses of cuttings in a commercial greenhouse. Nevertheless some protection for the wounded end is advisable. In England powdered sulfur is often used as a dip. In our opinion the hormone powder is a sort of insurance and does at least protect the wound from contamination.

The two principal brands of hormone powder are Rootone and Hormodin. They are available in variety stores and wherever plants are sold.

Removing Leaves

Since it is not good practice to bury the leaves at the base of our cutting, at least one row or node should be removed. Cut these leaves close to the stem but not so close as to remove the growth bud or miniature leaves in the axil. About ½ inch of stem, or more, must be buried in the vermiculite. If the leaves are very close together this will mean the cutting of two, three, or four leaves from the base of the cutting.

Removing leaves at the bottom of the cutting. The leaf buds are untouched. The ¾-inch stem is ample for planting.

Planting the Cuttings

Smooth out the vermiculite in the box. Dip the tip of the cutting in hormone powder, covering the stalk section that is bare. Shake off the excess. Poke a hole into the vermiculite with a dowel or stick and plant the cutting.

Cuttings should be planted very close together to save space. Don't worry about their having room for their roots. A well-planted cutting box should look like a solid mass of leaves unless, of course, you don't have enough to fill it.

Multiple Cuttings from the Same Branch

Besides the tip cutting, if the branch is long enough and has sufficient numbers of leaf nodes, you can make a series of cuttings from the same branch. Some plants put out long thin branches with many leaves, others do not. However, if you have taken multiple cuttings, be sure that you lay the ones that are not tip cuttings all facing in the same direction.

It is very easy to turn such cuttings the wrong way around and end up by planting them upside down. As they won't root that way, keep careful track of the direction of the stem.

Growing the Cuttings

Fit the lid on your cutting box and set it in reflected light at the window or at the ends of your light garden tubes. If the top of the box develops large drops of water all over it, you have overwatered your vermiculite. At most there should be a heavy haze on the inside of the plastic cover. Do not open the box for at least two weeks.

The temperature of your room should be at least 65° at all times during the incubation period.

Planting the cuttings. The tip of the stem has been dipped in the hormone powder, and we now just stick it into the vermiculite. For softer-stemmed plants a narrow hole must be made but the rosemary is tough.

The rosemary cuttings are in place and labeled along with the other contents of the bread box turned propagation box.

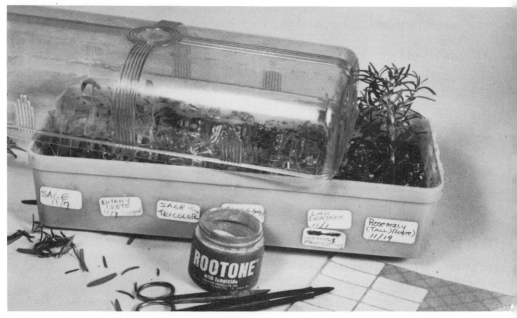

On top of the propagation box goes the transparent cover, not to be removed until the plants have rooted. Note the convenient stick-on labels of which we always keep a supply.

A typical rooted cutting. The vermiculite adheres to the roots and protects them in transplanting. *Lavandula dentata* cuttings in the background.

A cutting box with a different selection of herbs. Such boxes take up little room and are constantly reused.

We want this *Lavandula dentata* to grow in a columnar manner. When taking cuttings we therefore remove a side branch.

Our myrtle has only two branches. In order to make it more shrubby, we take a cutting from each of the branches. Where stems are leafy and nodes are close together, removing about one and a half inches of stem is advisable.

A single "crop" of cuttings from a propagation box. Plastic cups have been used because of a temporary shortage of regular plastic pots. New cuttings are already growing in the box.

A few sage cuttings can be accommodated in an old-fashioned glass. Another, slightly smaller one makes a perfect cover.

An old-fashioned glass with top.

Testing for Roots

After two weeks, open the cutting box and give one of the plants of each kind a gentle tug. If it offers resistance, pull it out. It should have a good ball of roots at the base. If it turns out that the rooting has just started, carefully poke it back into the vermiculite and close your box for another week, then repeat. No harm is done by this testing as the vermiculite is so loose.

The Rooted Cutting

As soon as your cutting has a good ball of root (½ inch or more all around), it can be potted up. The procedure is exactly the same as on page 63. The roots should not be washed, of course, and any vermiculite that adheres should be left on. However, the potting stick technique and the packing of the soil are the same.

Reusing the Propagation Box

Any time a cutting comes out another can go into the box. The vermiculite can be used over and over again, so that you may have a constant series of cuttings coming from the same box. Some cuttings of a variety may root faster than others. As you take them out of the box and pot them up, replace them with new ones.

The care of the cutting box is only a matter of keeping the vermiculite close to the same level and the moisture constant. If the cover is removed only when rooted cuttings are taken out, the moisture will remain the same for a long time. However, some allowance must be made for the amount of vermiculite taken out along with the roots. When you see that the level has dropped, add more vermiculite on top and a little moisture so that the condition of the box in both respects remains essentially the same.

10

Growing Herbs from Seed

Whenever possible start with plants rather than seed. The latter are even more incorrectly labeled than plants at nurseries. But there you can see, taste, and smell what you are buying, and a plant provides prompt cutting material which will develop more rapidly into a working plant than those from seed. However, some annuals are not available as plants, and this is sometimes true of the rarer exotic perennials. Also, when domestic seed catalogs do not offer what you need, you may be able to buy your requirements abroad.

Indoor seeding is not simpler than outdoor but it is much more reliable because of the controlled conditions in the house. Also we require so few plants that a few failed seeds are of no consequence. We use related methods depending on the type of plant and size of seed. In practice we rarely lose a seedling and have none of the damping-off (fungal disease of seedlings) problems that were so common formerly —due we suspect to cool temperatures.

For general growing conditions on windowsills and under lights, you should read those sections. Many herb seed kits are being sold without instructional material. The seeds are of the most common varieties and germinate reliably. But proper conditions, not suggested by the labeling of the kits, must be provided. Otherwise the plants will attenuate and soon die for lack of proper light and culture. We have heard continuous complaints on this score from unsuspecting would-be herb growers who thought they had brown thumbs when what was really lacking was the information that, as with all plants indoors, certain environmental conditions must be met or the plants will not flourish.

Large Seeds, Tropical Bean Seeds

When the seeds are over ¼ inch in diameter we fill a little pot with moist Rich or Lean Mix (it really doesn't matter), plant the seed just below the surface of the soil, cover the pot with a piece of glass or a sheet of plastic, place in a warm bright spot and wait for germination. Some of these seeds have very hard coats and may take weeks to come up. Some need only a soaking overnight in water to speed the process. With the really tough ones, apply a file to the side of the seed and scrape away a piece of the coating no bigger than a pinhead.

When the cotyledon appears aboveground and has spread its two halves, we dig up the plant, which has no root except a straight-down fleshy growth, and repot in a size that will accommodate it for a good part of its young life. The transplanting at this stage will not harm the plant. Usually the pot is about 1½ or 2 inches in diameter at the rim.

Medium-size Seeds

For these seeds we use a plastic bread box or a smaller transparent box with cover. We fill this to within an inch of the top with moist Lean Mix and poke the seeds one by one just below the surface. Then we spread a very thin coating of milled sphagnum moss over the surface. This will prevent damping-off of seedlings. If you don't have the moss it will be no tragedy. Spread a thin coating of vermiculite over the seeds instead.

This time we wait until there are both the cotyledons and a pair of leaves showing before transplanting to a small pot. You may have to cover the plant for a few days while it recovers. Use plastic sheet or an old-fashioned glass. Sometimes we place several small pots in a plastic storage box and leave the cover partly open.

Tiny Seeds

The very small seeds are the most difficult to handle, often because they are even hard to see clearly. Also the seedlings are very small and, though not always weak because of this fact, are difficult to handle without damage.

Make a mix consisting of even volumes of vermiculite and peat moss that has been carefully sieved or hand-manipulated to break up any lumps. Fill a transparent propagation box with part of the mix to within an inch of the rim. Moisten but do not soak it. Lay lengths of thin white string one inch apart straight across the surface of the soil to separate the rows. Label each planted area with a sticker on the outside of the box.

Take a tiny pinch of the seed and spread it as best you can between two lines of string. If the seed is very minute a pinch might mean a hundred seeds. So you may have to fold a piece of stiff white paper, drop your pinch onto it, shake back most of it into your seed pack and reserve no more than ten seeds for the box. Shake the paper along the row so that the seeds fall out gradually.

After the whole box is seeded, spread a thin film of dried mix or milled sphagnum over the surface. Close the box and place under the

lights or in good reflected light in the window. Warmth, between 70°
and 80° F, always aids germination.

When the seedlings start to come up, prepare another propagation
box with Lean Mix. As soon as the seedlings have two leaves grasp the
plant just below the surface of the soil with the points of tweezers, pull
it out and transfer it to the other box, plunging the little plant into the
soil. You will need a magnifying glass or, better still, an Opti-Visor
which permits you to operate with both hands. It may look like a case
of seedling murder but in practice it works beautifully. Even if the root
trails and you have to poke it in separately no harm is usually done. Now
the plants are spaced farther apart and have room to grow for a while.
Cover the propagation box and put under lights or in good reflected
light at a window. All the transplantings from a seedling box do not
have to take place at the same time but can be done in sequence as the
seedlings become ready. Keep your seedling box covered.

You won't kill the plants if you let them remain in the seedling box
for a longer period but you do run the risk of crowding and the development of a root system that is no longer supplied partly by food from
the seed itself. Transplanting can then become a more ticklish, if less
delicate, matter.

When your seedlings have several leaves and are an inch high,
transplant them to 2½-inch pots. The seedlings have become tender
because of the high humidity created by the cover. So, before transplanting, leave the cover partway open for two or three days. Dig up the
plants with a narrow indoor gardening trowel and follow the potting
procedures in our step-by-step pictures.

A small seed propagating box, seed packs, labels.

Labeling

Always label your plants, but especially seeds or cuttings in your
propagation box. Place the labels on the outside of the box. Self-stick-
ing ones are very convenient for the purpose.

Admittedly we, ourselves, are very careless about labeling. Although we have the excuse that we are experienced and know our plants

Adding a thin layer of milled sphagnum moss.

The seed box closed and ready to go on the windowsill or under lights.

well—usually—we have also made mistakes in the past and not been certain just exactly what plants we had until they bloomed. So get into the good habit right away.

The label should have: the Latin name of the plant
the variety if any, or a description
where bought or received and
date of planting.

For instance: *Rosmarinus officinalis*
Bowle's
Lauray (Nursery. See Sources for
Herb Plants and Seeds)12/21/74.

If we had no varietal name we might have described the unusual feature or the one that differentiated it from other like plants. For example—twin dble. mini-bracts. Meaning that the axils of the large leaves contained tiny double leaves on either side of the stem. Another variety had no bracts and a third had three joined bracts. By this means we can tell them apart and eventually identify them more precisely.

II

Training Herbs Indoors

As we grow herbs for their foliage rather than their flowers, it is essential in the house that we make their greenery as attractive as possible. There are a few herbs we grow purely for the "crop." These we may cut down drastically from time to time, thus automatically pruning them without any concern for aesthetic effect. But at least they will be made compact for a while and will appear undisciplined and overgrown for only a short time before we apply the scissors again.

However, the majority of our herbs, for instance those which are fragrant and which we do not cut for use, or the medicinals that we are not likely to use, if allowed to grow uncontrolled will either become leggy and unsightly or just sprawl. It is the nature of plants to keep on growing to their maximum natural height and to produce leaves and branches continuously in the process. This is part of the function also of reaching for light, and the development of the leaves nearest to the source of light is essential to the plant. In nature it must outgrow other, nearby, plants in season so that it will not remain continuously in their shade. Those plants that are creepers, instead of climbing, grow laterally, reaching out for new soil or also for a patch of sun.

In the process of growing and extending themselves, the lower leaves, or the leaves nearer the lower end of a stem or branch, usually dry out and die, a process that conserves strength for further growth. What remains behind is a swelling at the node to which the leaf was attached. This is called the leaf bud. And no further growth will take place at that point as long as the tips of stems and branches continue to put out new leaves.

Indoor growers, especially those with fluorescent light gardens, often complain about the loss of leaves on the lower parts of their plants, attributing it to the fact of growing on a windowsill or under the lamps. This occurs, however, just as much in the garden. The difference is not in the plant but our way of seeing it. In the garden we look down on plants of the size we grow indoors. We see the leafy tops and ignore the leafless stems below. In the house, on the other hand, we are on the same level and the effect is unsightly. Therefore, though it may be quite unnecessary outdoors, indoors we must take measures to do something about it. Plants in the house which lose their lower leaves have not been pruned properly or at all. If we prune them, we will have green leaves and branches and a shapelier, healthier-looking plant.

As usual, when we have a rule, there are some exceptions. One does not train a sarracinea or sundew or parsley because these are stemless plants, or *Mentha requienii* because it is so extremely small, or ginger because it has only a single leafy stem and further growth is from the root. However, any plant that branches normally from a stem is a candidate for training.

When we cut the growing tip of a plant, it signals the growth buds in the old axils of leaves farther down to get to work. If the plant is stopped from growing up, it begins to grow out. We call the cutting of the terminal leaf buds *nipping* because that is what we do with our fingers or with scissors. Sometimes the one or two tip leaves are easy to see and we snip them off with any length of stem down to the next leaf row. If the tip leaves are tightly clustered we may have to open the cluster and seek out the central leaves and remove them.

Cutting off the growing tip immediately activates the leaf buds at the base of the leaves just below and a branch starts to grow from each one. This reaction takes place not only at the tip of the plant stem, but at the tip of any branch which is similarly nipped. If the leaves at the growing tip and elsewhere are opposite each other, a branch will start from each leaf just below. If the leaves are alternate on the stem, at least one of the lower leaf buds is activated but usually two. In principle we gain two branches for each growing tip we cut.

The process goes a step further when we persistently remove the tips of the doubled branches. Not only does the doubling continue but the growing buds in the leaf axils further back on the plant also begin to leaf out or produce branches so that it assumes more and more a solid look of many small branches with numerous leaves and no bare stretches of stem. Since the roots as a result of our trimming have enough to do to maintain the mass of branches and leaves we have induced it to put out, it often resigns itself to remaining relatively inactive for a long time or resumes upward and outward growth very slowly. Thus very fleshy plants, with a habit of growing rapidly and becoming unsightly in a short time, can be trained through pruning carried on with persistence to remain compact and produce smaller leaves and shorter growths.

When a branch or stem has grown longer than we wish, we can take off much more than the tip if we choose, because we consider it will improve the shape. Instead of removing only the tip we can make our cut just above a leaf bud farther down the branch, perhaps several nodes or inches away from the tip. We then continue our shaping from that point. We may, in the process, remove sections of all the branches of a plant and end up with a much smaller, more compact one that, with further nipping as new branches develop, will be very much more dwarfed than its previous aspect.

Always make your cut directly above the node but not so close as to destroy the leaf bud without which you will have no branching. On the other hand, do not leave lengths of bare stem. They will die down to the node and persist as unsightly twigs.

With care you can combine pruning and cropping of herbs. Taking into consideration that your harvest is never very large indoors, if you do cutting for the kitchen carefully you can keep the plant shapely at the same time. Instead of an angular, chopped-up-looking plant, you can have one whose appearance improves every time you take leaves for use.

Even little herbs should be pruned. Each one will look best in proportion to its leaves and branches if it is kept within bounds. Thus, if you are persistent, a thyme can become a bushy little plant instead of a tangle of weak stems. Long branches can be removed for drying, and the remainder continues to grow as an attractive foliage plant.

How to Dry Herbs Indoors

Our recommendations for drying herbs will be very short because we have found only one method that works well in the house. The traditional method of hanging a bunch after tying it together with string fails because there is not sufficient air movement. The leaves often drop off on the floor and when the bunch is cut down, the leaves stripped and packed into jars, mold usually develops within a short time because the drying has not been perfect.

Spread your herb branches on a baking tin and set it in an oven with the door left wide open. It really does not matter at what temperature you set the oven thermostat. Leave the pan until the leaves and stems have become so dry that the former break at a touch and the latter snap as dead dried wood should. Then strip the leaves and store in a hermetically sealed container.

Trimmings from plants which you do not use in propagation can be dried and stuffed in a little jar like this one. It's a potpourri without recipe and smells as good.

12

The Cultural Herb List

Herb growing indoors is still in its infancy and will expand tremendously in the coming years. Many more plants will enter the repertory as we gain experience. In time the fragrant herbs will probably be as important as the culinary ones. Our list, therefore, is only suggestive of the future possibilities.

But our compilation is already a big advance over previous ones for indoor growing. In the past lists have concentrated on a relatively small number of kitchen herbs grown since time immemorial. The changes from one book to another were merely on the fringes—including a few herbs which are somewhat less common or less attractive. To fill in, plants were often included that were very unhappy in a home environment.

What makes our list partly a new one is its inclusion of medicinal plants, its widening of the base for fragrant plants, recommendation of tender varieties of standard herbs, and the inclusion of a few herbs from the subtropics or tropics. Because of the concentration in the past on outdoor gardening, a number of these plants were not considered suitable recommendations for the herb garden.

Tropical plants are particularly adapted to growing indoors as evidenced by the many kinds now being sold in garden centers and exotic florist shops. They were formerly considered rarities and were only to be seen in botanical gardens. Now they are among the most popular of houseplants, and the demand is greater than the supply. If you want to make a tropical herb garden, you need only select plants that have a legitimate medical history, are fragrant, or have been used in cooking. In doing so you will have satisfied all the requirements of the official definition of herb. We could have included many more were it not for the art of growing these plants being so new indoors that it would be premature to offer complete advice on their culture.

The character of our age is to offer us objects of interest from every corner of the world. Not long ago an art collection consisted entirely of examples from Europe and the Near East. Now we collect art from all the continents and every nation. Except as botanical specimens, plants from the far corners of the world did not enter into general horticulture until the beginning of the nineteenth century. Today we seek everywhere for those that suit our needs.

In colonial days it was a common practice to grow a few herbs near the house. As flower gardening became more general, herb gardening declined in popularity, becoming a specialty and a cult. Under the impact of urbanization the majority of our population no longer has a garden or, if the space is available, neither the time nor the means to keep one going. The new generation lives more and more in crowded suburbs or city apartments. And it is altogether appropriately timed that the flower garden and the herb garden, due to modern technology, now are possible indoors. Herb gardening in the home is here for good and will develop more and more with time as we find the precise plants best suited to our growing conditions and most attractive for the home.

Once you are interested in herbs there is much literature on the subject to which you can turn. Your curiosity may cause you to consult the catalogs of seedsmen and nurseries for exotic material. That is when you will be able to create your own, completely personal, list of indoor gardening herbs.

Cultural directions here are unavoidably repetitious. We are not growing most of these plants for flower. That requires different cultural procedures and is a greater challenge. The foliage plants are much easier.

Herb gardeners outdoors have long recognized that the form of many herbs—though not all—lends itself to ornamental shaping. That is an activity that should be carried on continuously indoors. Unless your herbs are an ornament they will not fit the neatness of your home. A sprawling, untidy herb garden has nothing to recommend it but its use, which is not very great. So learn, above all, how to control the form of your plants. If that skill is acquired, your herbs can be as beautiful as flowering plants indoors.

The fan-shaped leaves of lady's-mantle are unique among the herbs.

Alchemilla vulgaris. Lady's-mantle. **Rosaceae.** Europe. Perennial. Fluid extract used as an astringent and styptic.

In the moist woodland, where it grows, alchemilla will hardly attract your curiosity. You will not even notice it until it throws up stalks with tiny greenish or yellow flowers. Its only interest for us, therefore, is in the house where we can see its unusual and pretty leaves. These describe more than a half circle, are five- to seven-lobed, regularly toothed, and pleated like a fan. When they form a cluster on the top of a pot they can be very attractive indeed.

As a hardy perennial it prefers cool conditions and, as a plant of the forest floor, alchemilla will tolerate shade. Plant it in Lean Mix without lime in a rather deep pot and fertilize with a high nitrate solution, such as 30–10–10. Keep moist at all times. In the light garden it can be placed right at the ends of the tubes. In winter keep it a bit on the dry side.

A garlic clove will not last forever in a pot. But it is worth growing for the tasty greens which are more delicate than the bulb.

Allium. Onion. Garlic. Chives. *Liliaeceae.* Europe and Asia. Perennial Bulb. Culinary use.

We grow different kinds of onions in the house not for the bulbs but the leaves. The bulbs require more space both to grow to proper size and to have enough of them to make growing worthwhile. So our consideration is how much leaf is produced. We all know that chives are a standard kitchen windowsill plant and that we don't use the bulbs anyway. But it is a somewhat different matter when we grow a top onion or garlic. All the leafy parts of these plants are tasty but the differences in flavor are virtually impossible to define.

A problem with the onions is that they go dormant in nature and also like a rest in the house. A couple of weeks on a windowsill in the late fall or a trip to the refrigerator gives them a new lease on life. The trouble is that we do not as yet have much experience with these plants, except the chives. But it is not at all unlikely that with a proper regimen we can keep them going constantly. This depends partly on their getting enough fertilizer, as they are voracious consumers.

The onions like a sandy, well-drained soil with some fibrous content. They detest standing water yet need lots of it to keep growing. A bulb bowl is often recommended but this hardly provides room for a rather extensive root system. They need lots of sun to bloom but if we are satisfied with the leaves, which is all we are likely to get anyway, they can take shade. Indoors leaves tend to be soft and are easily knocked down and crimped. We can avoid this by continuous cropping which is, after all, what they are there for in the first place. Anyway this is how we do it.

Seeding. We never use the true onion seed as growth takes far too long and handling the plants from pot to pot becomes a chore. Either we plant the full-grown onion, a clove as in the case of garlic, onion sets —which are seedling onions or offsets—or plants, as with chives. The production of leaf is very quick.

Soil. Lean mix with lime.

Pots. If we start out with small sets we plant several in a 4-inch or bigger pot. Whole onions or garlic cloves go into their individual pots. These should be minimum 4-inch diameter and 4 inches deep. The small chives are clustered and take up little room. Larger chive kinds will go two or three to a 4-inch pot.

Sets are planted just below ground level but whole onions and cloves are put only halfway into the soil. The larger chives should always have some of their sheath above ground.

Light. Poor light will make for slower soft growth but, since we do not usually want to use premium sunlight areas for these plants, they have to do their best at the side of a window or at the ends of the tubes.

Water. The main thing is not to waterlog the plants. Provided the soil is sufficiently granular in texture, and drainage is first rate, this should be sufficient. Planting the onion in a hole lined with vermiculite or, even better, perlite, will protect it from rot.

Temperature. Alliums prefer it rather cool, but they will take the summer heat if the soil is not soggy.

Fertilizer. We use high nitrate fertilizer, 30–10–10 or a slow-release fertilizer such as Osmocote or Mag-Amp.

Cutting. Cutting back the plants encourages growth and should be carried on regularly. Cut to a couple of inches from the top of the bulb. As leaves have a tendency to elongate after cutting, you can avoid crimping and excessive length by cutting off four or five inches of the tip. Don't let any of the leaves become dried out. Cut them long before this is likely to happen.

Do not let the soil dry out. That will stop growth and may suggest to the bulb that it is time for dormancy. If that happens, you will have to keep it dry. The sign will be when no new growth appears. Reduce or eliminate watering and set the plant aside for a couple of months. When you bring it back into action, water very gently until leaves are growing well, otherwise the bulb will rot out.

Allium cepa viviparum. Egyptian Top Onion.

The top onion is only a variety of the cultivated vegetable onion, which has innumerable strains. It is peculiar among these, however, in propagating mainly from bulblets that form at the top of a central stem. The underground bulbs just go soft and give out after a while. So to perpetuate this onion you have to get that central top growth. This is not too easy in the house, where the sun is not as strong as outdoors.

For best results put your pot of bulblets in your best light and keep moist but not soggy. As leaves develop good length—a foot or more— lop them off for cooking. If you get some tops and have an excess, you can use them too for flavoring stews, soups, and sauces. If you don't, buy another packet of bulblets for seeding.

Allium sativum. Garlic.

The advantage of garlic is that it is always available at your vegetable store. There are many varieties including those purplish ones. The leaves are wider than most, up to an inch, and can be over a foot in length. Break off a fat clove and plant halfway into your mix and water moderately. The leaves taste like garlic—surprise.

If your garlic grows well it may even produce offsets, which can be broken off and started separately. You won't get a lot but you can have fun watching its leaves grow and surprising your friends.

A small pot of chives. Roots are already showing below, and it really needs something deeper in order to grow and multiply. Notice the oxalis at the base, an unwelcome gift from the farm. This is the weedy type of oxalis that must be eradicated wherever it appears in pots indoors.

Allium schoenoprasum. Chive.

Don't try to grow this from seed. It takes a couple of years to get anywhere. Buy a pot from the vegetable store in the spring and try to keep going from then on.

It is usually jammed into some particularly bad sandy soil. Break up the cluster and plant in separate pots with room to grow. Use new Lean Mix to fill out the empty spaces. Water well and set in the window or under the lights. Fertilize often and cut often to keep it active.

If your chive plants reach a point where they refuse to grow leaves anymore, let them dry out completely and put them in the refrigerator for a month. Then bring them back to the warmth again and water slightly. If they start to grow, go back to regular watering. If they don't budge, put them back in the refrigerator for another few weeks (or give up and buy another pot). Any time the cluster gets too big just divide it into separate pots. With good care and luck you should have chives to cut most of the year.

Garlic chives after a cutting. Far better to grow from seed and harvest the babies.

Allium tuberosum. Garlic Chives.

You can treat the seed of this onion almost the same as mustard and cress. Buy a good quantity and plant thickly on the surface of Lean Mix in a shallow container—a 4-inch azalea shape (broad and shallow) will do. Cover the seed with a thin coat of mix. The crop will be a thick one. When it reaches 2 inches in height pull up the whole contents of the pot, wash it, and store it in a plastic bag. It will provide you with enough chives for salads and cooking for weeks. Meanwhile start another pot.

This onion or a close relative can be bought almost year round at your neighborhood Japanese or Chinese grocery. It comes in bunches, bare root. When you get home remove the tops right down to the white part and store for use. The bulbs can be planted in Lean Mix fairly close together in a shallow plastic pot. Place in the window or under lights and cut the leaves as they grow. They won't last forever but you will have a good harvest for many weeks. When they start to look tired, pull them all up and use them in your cooking.

Some other alliums are:

A. fistulosum, the Welsh Onion. Requires very limy soil. Treatment is the same as for the top onion.

A. ascalonicum. Shallot. There is much confusion about the botany of this plant and many plants and seeds are sold that don't have the rich flavor of this culinary superherb at its best. Success in multiplying the tubers indoors is rare indeed, and the leaves are not worth the trouble. Try planting a few of these small onions in an azalea pot in a very sunny window. If you win out, it will be a real triumph. When the plant stops growing, dry out the bulbs, place in a plastic bag (or use them in cooking), and store for at least six weeks in the refrigerator.

There are lots of decorative onions for the garden available from seedsmen. When you can get the sets (the seedling bulbs), you can try your hand. Not all are particularly tasty or aromatic.

Aloe vera will soon develop new growths from the base and become a mass of spikes which can be separated and potted up. It's hard to believe that this innocent-looking plant is credited with so many medicinal and cosmetic virtues.

Aloe vera. Aloe. Barbados Aloe. **Liliaceae.** Mediterranean. Perennial. Medicinal.

The aloe is in vogue to such an extent that all kinds of beneficial claims are made for it. The juice of the leaves is used as a purgative and to cure sunburn and relieve insect bites. Lately it has turned up in cosmetics as an improver of skin conditions and remover of blemishes. According to *Potter's Cyclopaedia*, aloes "given to mothers—causes purging in the suckling infant." He lists as medicinal herbs, in addition to *A. vera, A. chinensis, A. perryi, A. spicata,* and *A. ferox.*

In true herbal manner we need not be particular about which aloe we grow as long as it is attractive and does well in the house. As these plants are of tropical origin they are not to be found in northern herb gardens. So here we have an enrichment with which you can also get rid of your blemishes—if you have any.

The aloes are fleshy succulents with rosettes of thick, long-pointed leaves that are in some species bare, in others edged with spines. Some develop stems and have leaves in whorls, and there are those which grow quite huge in size. For the house the smaller kinds are preferred, and among these are many which are most ornamental. *Aloe vera* is a plain type, green, with at most a few teeth. But there are beautiful mottled and striped species and hybrids.

Aloes are among the easiest of houseplants to grow. They seem to be almost impervious to mistreatment and produce offsets in great quantity, which need only be detached from the parent plant and potted up as they usually have roots of their own.

88

They will do equally well in Succulent or Lean Mix, do not require your best sun, and are not fussy about watering except in very cool weather. They can go without it for a long time or you can wet them along with your nonsucculent plants. Just don't have them sitting in water.

They do flower—sometimes with very long inflorescences of pendent yellow tube flowers. But you are not likely to see that in the house. At least that is not our experience. However, we know of others who have reported bloom on some of the smaller plants. It is not impossible in a bright window by any means, but a bit more difficult under lights.

As these plants are very prolific and can tolerate pot binding, keep them in the smallest pot you can until they hang over the sides. They look very well that way too, when there are a number of offsets with their leaves all entangled.

Anyway you could have a whole herb garden of aloes, there being so many different kinds from all over Africa and the Mediterranean. Among the prettiest are *A. humilis, A. aristata, A brevifolia, A. ciliaris, A. ferox*—one of the true medicinals, very thorny but attractive with red flowers—*A. mitriformis*, and the quite gorgeous stripy *A. variegata*, whose leaves overlap in a most interesting way. Succulent nurseries carry many more and you can pick your own according to your liking.

Alpinia purpurata is one of the showiest of the decorative gingers.

Alpinia. Decorative Ginger. **Zingiberaceae.** East Indies. Perennial. Aromatic foliage and roots with somewhat ginger flavor. Also medicinal.

We grow alpinias principally as ornamentals. But they come by their herbal credentials honestly, for *Alpinia galangais* is credited with a whole medicine cabinet full of virtues, and Potter calls it *Alpinia officinarum.* The leaves have a very pleasant gingery odor. So here we have another tropical plant, fine for the house, of which there are a number of species for our modern herb garden. In fact one of our best tropical nurseries lists *Alpinia purpurata* as a herb.

These plants require an azalea-type pot (broad and shallow), Rich Mix without lime, temperatures of 65° F or higher, even moisture, and the use of a balanced fertilizer. They will do well in partial sun or under the lights.

In appearance they are cane plants with alternate whorled longish leaves which are often prettily variegated. They grow, under good culture up to two feet in height, but can be trimmed to smaller size, and they increase by root growth and can be divided whenever you please by simply cutting the root in sections.

A. purpurata, red ginger, has bright red bracts on a leafy stem.

A. sanderae and *A. speciosa variegata* are variegated creamy or white with green stripes.

This is not an easy plant to bloom in the house but well worth while if you can do it. They come in hanging clusters of yellow or white marked with red.

Buy plants from a tropical nursery.

The aromatic leaves are the attraction of cardamon, which resembles a broad-leaved ginger plant.

Amomum cardamon. Cardamon. **Zingiberaceae.** East Indies. Perennial. The seeds used in baking and Indian dishes. Leaves aromatic.

The alphabetical arrangement is responsible for bringing another member of the ginger family right after *Alpinia*. Cardamon is much better known and has many uses. Other species of Amomum also have medicinal properties. The culture is the same as for alpinia and the aromatic leaves are the attraction. But it is not likely to bloom for you, and must be considered a pure foliage plant in the house. Seeds that are viable can be purchased but you are better off starting with a plant.

Pretty scarlet pimpernel comes in an equally striking blue. A little crawling plant, it is a gem for a sunny window.

Anagallis arvensis. Scarlet Pimpernel. ***Primulaceae.*** Europe. Annual. Medicinal.

We are pleased that the scarlet pimpernel has immigrated to our shores. In New England you can see it on the Cape growing between cracks in the pavement and displaying the bluest of flowers alternately with a matte but rich brick red. We've seen both colors on the same plant. But you can buy seeds of either color. Plant them both, for the contrast is unusually charming.

This harmless-looking plant is described by the herbalists as useful "in dropsy, rheumatic affections, hepatic and renal complaints." But to be used with caution. We have never seen it in an herb garden, which is a shame for it is also a weather prophet, and will tell you when to head for the shed. The flowers, it is said, never open on a rainy day and foretell a shower by closing in advance. In the old country it's called poor man's weatherglass. You can't resist something like that.

The form of the plant is creeping or straggiing, and the colorful flowers and their size are the only beauty. But they are worth the effort.

Plant the seed directly in moist Lean Mix with lime in a shallow pot. If you have a 6-incher, plant about a dozen evenly spaced seeds just below the surface. Cover the pot with a sheet of plastic or glass and set under the lights or in partial sunlight. When the shoots appear, remove the glass and water from below just enough to keep the soil moist. Set the pot in your brightest light and let the plant run. If there are too many seedlings in the pot, just pull out the excess. Fertilize with a high phosphate–potash solution.

Seed can be planted at any time of the year but you will need at least two plantings to have year-round bloom. Very often they seed themselves and you can start new pots with these plants.

The feathery green leaves of dill are too insubstantial to permit growing much of a crop indoors. But if you keep a pot growing, you will have just what you need for a special fish or sauce.

Anethum graveolens. Dill. ***Umbelliferae.*** Europe. Biennial. Culinary.

Oh, if one could only grow enough dill in the house. It is such a wonderful herb in cooking, with a flavor which is unique and indescribable. It is superb in soup, for flavoring fish, the fine fresh cuttings in sour cream or sweet cream for vegetables. It is so delicate that it must never receive much cooking and should be tossed in at the last moment. Dillseed is used in baking and pickling. But you won't get seed from your plants in the house no matter how much you try.

Unfortunately, it takes a lot of dill to keep the kitchen supplied, and most homes just don't have the space. Also it must be treated as an annual and its useful life is not too long—say a few months. So we have to sow at least four times a year to get a continuous supply.

Provided with a rather delicate taproot for so large a plant (it grows to two feet given the chance), it must be sowed right in the pot. Use a 6-inch azalea pot filled with Lean Mix and lay about twelve seeds, evenly distributed, on the surface. Then press each one in a bit. Put plastic wrap over the top of the pot and set in a dark place preferably at around 65° F. Germination takes place in about two weeks.

Dill will not grow with the same vigor indoors as out but, since we are only interested in the leaves, the single pot may provide a respectable bunch. Set the pot in good sunlight or center under the lights and keep moist. Fertilize with high nitrate formulas (30–10–10 or similar). When the plants are several inches high, and if they should become bushy, they can be thinned out. This will give you fresh dill from the discards and you can start cutting back the rest. Always leave about 4 inches of stem. Less damage and more branching will occur if you trim only a few inches of leaf tips at a time. By alternating two or three pots you should have a fair supply. After the stem thickens it eventually becomes woody and unproductive and, by that time, your second pot should be ready. The first one can then be replanted.

The strains for growing leaves are different from those for seeds. The German Chrestensens Herkules is a leaf type. Check with your seedsman for you will have much better results with the leaf type.

93

In the early stages of growth, chamomile forms a fascinating rosette of stems and leaves.

Anthemis nobilis. Roman Chamomile. ***Compositae.*** Europe. Perennial. Medicinal.

Drink chamomile tea, made of flowers or leaves or both, every day and you will live to a hundred. Excellent, saith the herbalist, as an external application for toothache.

Who says that you can't grow this sovereign herb indoors? Under fluorescent light it will bloom nicely. And, if you buy seed or plants of the flore-pleno, or double flowering, kind, you will delight in the neat little white buttons on one-foot plants with feathery leaves. In the window the chances are much less of blooming this plant unless the season is very sunny.

Although botanically a perennial, it is of the hardy type that requires not so much a freeze as a different habit to grow a long time indoors. Some perennials develop a productive woody structure that continues with leaves and flowers year after year. Anthemis is after all a daisy, and its single stem loses its productivity in a season and has to die down to the root to renew itself. So, in practice, we have to grow it as an annual. This is perfectly satisfactory as we can plant it at any time of year indoors under lights.

There is another element of the effect of indoor growing on such plants that is both new and interesting. Outdoors we always grow them from seed and indoors we also start them that way. But as the maturing plant branches we can cut some off and use them as cuttings. They will root quickly and well. So it is possible to have a continuous flow of plants without seeds and the succession is much more rapid and pain-less.

Plant a few seeds of anthemis in a propagation box. They will germinate in about five days. When they have four leaves, transplant to 3- or 4-inch pots in Lean Mix. The 3-incher will hold one and the 4-, two plants. Water frequently but don't let the pots stand in it.

Chamomile, *Anthemis nobilis,* in flower. If you wish to have the flowers, you will find it difficult to keep the plant compact at the same time.

The foliage of chervil is even lacier than parsley, and the flavor much more delicate. You can see that it takes a number of chervil plants to grow enough for the salad or the sauce.

Anthriscus cerefolium. Chervil. *Umbelliferae.* Southern Europe. Annual. Culinary.

Chervil is often described as a superior parsley, which it is not. The similarity goes no further than the appearance and, even in this respect, it is much more feathery than parsley. Parsley has a slightly bitter, dry flavor, while chervil has the most delicate of those anise-licorice tastes that are typical of so many of the carrot family. The French value it highly but we cannot buy it in our shops and, in spite of its fame, it is little grown in America. It is essentially a salad flavorant or to be finely snipped and sprinkled on cooked dishes at the last moment.

A typical feathery-leafed relative of dill and fennel, it has a delicate root and must be planted where it is to grow. The seed being viable for only a short time must be bought in season. This creates difficulties for the indoor grower unless he can grow his own seed, which is highly unlikely. Be sure that the seed you buy is fresh from the source.

Plant below ground in Lean Mix in azalea-type pots, window boxes, or trays and figure on a seed every 3 inches. This way the plants will not grow as big but you can have a small forest for cutting. Germination is rapid and within a few weeks you can start to cut.

One reason why chervil is not as popular here as in England is that it dislikes intense summer heat and will tolerate full sun only if the air is cool. It doesn't like excessive humidity either. Thus the stories that it is so easy to grow are from those who have the right climate and the complaints from those who do not.

Once the chervil is up, though, give it your best sun or artificial light and try to keep the air cool by means of fans in hot weather. Maintain moderate moisture at all times.

Rosemary as decorative setting.

Herbs on tray. Back row left to right: rosemary, lady's-mantle, pineapple sage. Front row: santolina, curry plant, artemisia.

Table setting.

Variegated mint.

Herb garden on kitchen workspace under lights.

Kitchen cabinet herb garden.

Monarda didyma. *Oswego Tea (a native herb).*

Transplanted seedlings.

Medieval garden at The Cloisters in New York.

Cistus salvifolius. *Rockrose.*

Aquilegia canadensis. *Common columbine of America.*

Aquilegia vulgaris. *Common columbine of Europe.*

Cichorium intybus. *Chicory.*

Cistus laurifolius. *Rockrose.*

Arctostaphylos uva-ursi. *Bearberry.*

Origanum vulgare. *Wild oregano.*

Mitchella repens. *Partridgeberry.*

Drosera rotundifolia. *Sundew.*

Punica granatum. *Dwarf pomegranate.*
Flower.

Rosa rugosa. *Wild Rose.*

Rosa canina. *Wild Rose.*

Tricolor sage.

Taraxacum officinale. *Dandelion.*

Sanguisorba minor. *Salad Burnet.*

Aquilegia canadensis and ***vulgaris.*** Columbine (Common American and Common European). ***Ranunculaceae.*** Perennial. Medicinal.

Nobody uses columbine for medicine today (that we know of) but once upon a time the powdered dried plant was made into a hot toddy and produced perspiration—which hot toddies of all kinds do anyway. Probably its chief recommendation to herbal medicine was the disagreeable odor and bitter taste. What could be better?

A friend of ours bought a plant of *A. canadensis,* the one with the beautiful yellow and red flowers, from a wild flower nursery and let it loose in his cool cellar fluorescent light garden. He reports that the plants have bloomed and seeded themselves at all times of the year. Since he had a raised bench with garden loam, the plants took care of themselves. They require limy soil, rich and porous. Rich Mix with lime will do and keep it very moist. If you have the cool conditions and the lights you can grow them nicely. *A. vulgaris* is the blue species, with shorter spurs, and there are varieties that bloom white or pink.

Arctostaphylos uva-ursi. Bearberry. ***Ericaceae.*** North Asia and America. Evergreen perennial. Medicinal.

A medicine man's delight. Particularly good for the gravel and in cases of menorrhagia (*you* look that up). It's a beautiful creeping plant with succulent-looking stems and leaves and lovely white lantern flowers with pink tips. Growing from seed is not advisable, as it requires a cold period of definite length to germinate. But you can buy plants from wild flower nurseries. They will do best in a cool cellar light garden, planted in azalea pots of Lean Mix without lime. In the fall, stick pot and all in the refrigerator and leave it there for two months. It will enjoy the coolth and provide you with spring flowers. The red berries, which are aromatic, are the bonus. Cuttings can be rooted. Give the plant good sun or artificial light.

On the West Coast there are a number of species of arctostaphylos, some of them low plants and some pretty big shrubs. We have no experience with them, but one or another may prove a good houseplant. West Coasters should try them out if they haven't already.

We have also not experimented as yet with bearberry in a terrarium and suspect that the light may be too low. Here, again, it is worth experimenting. Bear in mind that we are all still babes in the woods regarding the potential of innumerable plants for the house and that it will require years of trial before some categories have been well explored for indoor use.

Since wormwood is not used as a vermifuge, we must assume that the name applies to the manner of growth. This is a winter plant from a greenhouse and is properly wormy looking.

Artemisia absinthium. Absinthe. Wormwood. ***Compositae.*** Europe. Perennial. Medicinal.

If you grow your own wormwood, you can make your own absinthe. Although more effective ways of "taking a trip" have been found, this plant is the source of a drink celebrated in story and art (Degas, Picasso). Actually its effect is mainly narcotic, but can be habit forming.

A small shrub, which may grow with time to four feet, *A. absinthium* exists on very poor soil, likes sun, and doesn't require either much water or much of any fertilizer. This is, therefore, another plant tolerant of being starved. Keep it small so that its rather pretty serrate and cut leaves will show to best advantage and it will develop a trunk. Give it Lean Mix with some lime. Grow like a bonsai for form rather than size. The leaves are aromatic and very bitter to the taste, so there is little likelihood that your child will get itself a jag chewing them. Buy plants.

Southernwood makes an attractive foliage plant. Plant several in a pot and cut them back when they grow about 6 inches high. You will have a beautiful mound of foliage in the pot if you are persistent in pruning.

Artemisia abrotanum. Southernwood. Old Man. ***Compositae.*** Europe. Perennial. Medicinal.

Of the artemisias that are valued as silvery grey border plants in the herb garden, *A. abrotanum* is the most common. During its long European history, it has also been used as a flavoring for foods and, distilled, as an astringent and bitter. The leaves have a delicate scent of lemon.

Southernwood has a very short history as an indoor plant. We have been growing it without difficulty but have not achieved what we believe is entirely possible and certainly desirable, pots containing mounds of the foliage under perfect control. In our desire to ensure its living with us we have let it get a bit out of hand. If you can acquire very young plants, we are sure that it is only necessary to prune early and often to produce branching and to succeed with the mounds.

This is a plant that can be carried from year to year and should be treated essentially like *A. absinthium.*

Southernwood is related to a number of other artemisias that have been developed purely for ornamental grey edging in gardens. Such plants as *A.* 'Silver Mound,' which we illustrate, make fine modest foliage plants for the house. The distinction of the artemisias and santolinas is that nurserymen have been working for generations to make them more compact and to increase their silvery look. The result is a group of plants quite different from anything else in the world of cultivated plants.

A very small pot of *Artemisia* 'Silver Mound,' one of a number of purely ornamental artemisias for edging in the garden. On the windowsill it can become a neat lush mound of pure silver.

Close-up of *Artemisia* 'Silver Mound.'

Tarragon is properly upstanding in summer though a bit shaky on its pins. You will be lucky if you have this much growing in winter. Keep it rather dry for a while and subject it to a two-week freeze. New growth here is just starting at the base.

Artemisia dracunculus. Tarragon. **Compositae.** Europe. Perennial. Culinary.

We deal with tarragon separately because it has no peer as a culinary herb. There are few scents in the world more delicious than that which assails our olfactory prominences when we open a jar of dried tarragon leaves. It is like the sweetest of new-mown hay on a dewy, moonlit night. How is it that no one has made a perfume of it? The subtle, unique flavor "makes" a Sauce Béarnaise, many a stew and, among others, sauces for veal and chicken. Contrary to some authorities, we do not value the fresh herb. For us the dried condition is far superior.

However—it is a recalcitrant plant. It must be bought as a plant because true tarragon does not, apparently, set seed in this country. It is supposed to in France and certainly our summers are hotter than those of England where they have the same problem. In buying your plant be careful that the leaves have that delicate anise flavor. The real strength only comes out in drying. There are seed-grown plants and seed sold as tarragon, legitimately. They are not, however, the true-blue original but one of the varieties which are virtually tasteless.

All the potted plants we have seen have been scrawny. Brought into the house and transplanted to a decent soil, it will grow well in a sunny window or under lights until tall. Thereupon it begins to fade, no matter how warm your home temperature remains. If kept indoors and watered, the plant will rot rapidly. The only solutions are either put the pot out of doors (on the outside of the window for instance), for two weeks of frost, or set it in the refrigerator for about a month. Then it may start to come back.

When the leaves and stems start to go, cut them down to within an inch or two of the ground. This will encourage new growth—if you get new growth. The plant, once it starts up again, should be divided by breaking it into two parts and repotted after removing the soil.

Plant tarragon in Lean Mix with a full complement of lime. Water well and fertilize lightly is the rule. Give the plant your best light on windowsill or in the light garden. Usually a deep 4- or 5-inch pot is needed.

Take and plant cuttings in August. They will grow slowly but stay green all winter.

Sweet woodruff looks big in the illustration but is only a few inches high and weak-stemmed once it is mature. Little white flowers are produced in late spring. It requires a short freeze in winter to recover and grow again. Nice for a small pot.

Asperula odorata. Sweet woodruff. ***Rubiaceae.*** Europe. Perennial. Culinary.

This is a widespread little perennial in northern Europe, with very fragrant leaves and small white flowers, growing about 8 inches on single leafy stems and spreading by underground roots. It is used dry in sachets and potpourris and lends a nauseatingly cloying flavor and odor to May Wine. However, it requires a freeze in winter.

Over summer it will do all right in a 4-inch pot, or a larger azalea pot indoors as it tolerates shade. The soil must be as acid as possible. This is the exception where some woods soil such as that in which partridgeberry and wintergreen grow would be better than our Rich Mix and high nitrate fertilizer. Keep it as cool as possible. For this reason cellar conditions are about as near to right for it as we are likely to come. Of course, air conditioning helps. Buy plants.

There are woodruffs from southern Europe that are equally small or smaller, and these probably would make better houseplants. The original will do all right for a season provided you have the above conditions and, in the fall, you can put it outside the window to spend the winter.

102

This relatively rare *Azara* is an exquisite shrub for the house.

Azara celastrina and ***dentata. Flacourtiaceae.*** Chile. Perennial. Fragrant flowers.

This is an attractive shrub which grows to twelve feet but can be kept small by pruning. As long as a shrub has small leaves this is usually not too difficult, and those of azara are glossy and only 1½ inches long. The small fuzzy golden flowers are intensely fragrant. *A. microphylla,* with which we have no experience, is mentioned by some writers. As the species name implies, this has still smaller leaves.

Azara will grow in Rich Mix with lime, first in a 4-inch pot and later, perhaps, in a small tub. But with careful training it can be kept miniature for any length of time. Give it moderate light, even moisture, and high nitrate fertilizer. After blooming, cut down on the watering and keep barely moist for a couple of months.

Bellis perennis. English Daisy. **Compositae.** Western Europe. Biennial. Medicinal.

Bellis perennis is a garden flower that does not look well in the garden. Somehow the effect is always drab. On the other hand, because of scale, it looks great in the house. Flowers, according to the variety, vary from one to three inches across. The "carpet" types are best.

It is rather surprising to learn that this ordinary-looking daisy is, according to Leyel *(Green Medicine)*, "so valuable that it is a constant source of amazement for it cures pains that have been untouched by other remedies." Read on.

Compact forms grow six inches high, have crinkled close-fitting green leaves and nice double chrysanthemumlike flowers in white or pink. In the house the seed may be sown any time of year, will germinate in about eight days, but will grow to blooming size rather slowly. Plant the seed directly into 4-, 6-, or 8-inch pots. The 4-inch will hold a single plant, the rest in proportion. Use Rich Mix and fertilize with high nitrate solutions. Keep moderately moist and in a sunny position or directly under the center of the lights. Later on they can be moved to the side when well grown. They prefer cool temperatures in the house. Start a new pot every four months.

Cedronella triphylla. False Balm of Gilead. **Labiatae.** Canary Islands. Fragrant leaves. Perennial shrub.

This is a small shrub with typical toothed minty leaves and racemes of typical pink minty flowers. The leaves are aromatic with a warm, slightly oily, slightly lemony scent.

Brittonastum mexicanum, which is sometimes sold as a cedronella, is a smaller plant with simple 2½-inch leaves and 1-inch spike flowers— rather the prettier of the two.

Grow these in Lean Mix and keep moderately moist in good light. Trimming and shaping as they grow will keep them bushy. Try to maintain them in a five-inch pot. They will stay more dwarfed, and you can still enjoy the balsamic leaves.

Chimaphila umbellata and **maculata.** Pipsissewa. Spotted Wintergreen. **Pyrolaceae.** North America. Perennial. Medicinal.

Of these two closely related plants, only *C. umbellata* is listed in most of the herbals, where it is credited with virtues in the treatment of rheumatic and kidney affections. "It is especially valuable in scrofulous debility" (Potter). Anybody who is scrofulous these days should not give up hope. We list *C. maculata,* the spotted wintergreen, with some reason since among its common names in various country regions are rheumatism root, dragon's tongue, wild arsenic, and ratsbane. That is a combination which is irresistible.

These plants have often been collected in the past for use in woodsy terrariums, a practice being curtailed by a natural desire to preserve the wild plants. However, cultivated ones can be bought from wild flower nurseries.

Pipsissewa displaying its exquisite flowers. They are waxy white in petal and the fringe and center are soft pink. It requires acid soil which is very well drained but can grow in rather deep shade.

In a terrarium they grow best in very acid soil, with a large admixture of hemlock or pine needles. Coolness, some shade, and even moisture are required. There should be no fertilizer. On the whole it would be better to use acid soil brought from the woods than one of our mixes. But Rich Mix will be suitable in a pinch. If you wish to carry the plants from year to year, it will be advisable to set the terrarium out of doors (with overhead protection) to freeze in winter for at least a month.

The two plants do well with other woodland herbs, such as partridgeberry and wintergreen.

Pipsissewa has leaves broader and rounded at the tip. *C. maculata*'s leaves are long-pointed and have a white stripe down the middle. The leaves of both are whorled and the flowers are hanging clusters of white wax with pinky centers and a fine fresh fragrance.

No other member of the citrus group quite compares with *Choisya* for flowering and classical form of the dark leaves.

Choisya ternata. Mexican Orange. ***Rutaceae.*** Mexico and California. Perennial. Fragrant flowers.

Choisya is an interesting alternative to the true citrus plants of which it is a relative. It is a shrub, up to ten feet in height, which, like so many other tropical shrubs and small trees, can be grown in anything from a medium-size pot to a good-size tub depending on your space and setting. Choisya will do well on a sun porch or by a bright window.

The distinction of the plant, which has leaves with three leaflets, are its clusters of white flowers, over an inch across, with a fragrance close to vanilla. When the plant is well grown, the flowering can be almost continuous.

Grow it from a small plant, repotting in Rich Mix if possible, and watering and fertilizing well. It likes a high nitrate fertilizer.

Cuttings from young wood root easily.

You will not want a large pot of costmary since its uses in the home are almost nonexistent nowadays. But it makes a pretty foliage plant when small. How different the leaves of these herbs are from our other houseplants and what a decorative contrast they create!

The long petiole and leaf of costmary-alecost.

Chrysanthemum balsamita. Costmary. Alecost. *Compositae.* Asia. Perennial. Flavor, fragrance, and medicine.

In the house costmary is interesting mainly for its long oval leaves on very long petioles. The leaves have a minty odor and can be used in salads, though a little bitter. An ointment was formerly made of the crushed leaves and was considered soothing for burns and bruises. Allowed to run, it will reach two to three feet in height and produce small yellow few-rayed daisy flowers.

Costmary has the habit of growing side shoots, which can be cut free from the parent plant with some root. Pot these up in Lean Mix with lime and place in a sunny window or under lights. If they start to develop stems, trim back and keep the plants dwarfed. In the house a 4- or 5-inch pot is ample, and there is no reason to take up additional room with a plant that has not too much to recommend it. Fertilize with a balanced formula and dry out a bit between waterings.

Cichorium intybus. Chicory. *Compositae.* Europe. Perennial. Medicinal and flavorant.

It is hard to believe that that weed with the deep blue daisy flowers (one of the few blues among our "wild" plants in the East) which grows on road edges in the country, often cropped by the mower or crushed by car wheels, is the same whose roots are used to make a coffee substitute, while its nearest relative, *Cichorium endivia,* produces the elegant blanched salad and braising vegetable called endive. But so it is. Which only proves that in plants as in people, genius wears no particular garb.

Herb gardeners don't bother about this "weed," which blooms much more prettily than most of their favorites and is altogether easy to grow outdoors. You can't buy plants and don't need them. Just collect the seeds in July, August, or September. Good-size cuttings root rather easily.

This leggy plant has a big coarse taproot that is dried, ground, and roasted for French coffee. Therefore it needs a deep pot though a 4-incher will do for a start. Plant a seed or two in such a pot with Lean Mix without lime. Water plentifully but don't drown. Give it the sunniest position in your window or under lights and, as soon as it has a few leaves, begin to trim it back so that it branches a lot more than in nature. In this way you can produce a feathery-leafed compact plant which will bloom in due time. Feed with high nitrate fertilizer as it prefers an acid soil. If you produce some root, read up on chicory production and make yourself a cup.

Cistus. Rockrose. *Cistaceae.* Southern Europe. Perennial. Fragrant leaves.

Seeing rockroses for the first time on Mediterranean hillsides we took them for true roses, since at a distance they are almost identical in appearance with the single wild ones. They have a bushy, rather columnar growth and, in season, produce quantities of 3-inch white or pink flowers which last only a day.

We suggest growing these plants in the herb garden only for the fragrant leaves, as you will have difficulty getting them to bloom. The leaves are hairy, sticky, and crumpled, producing a heavy incense odor on warm days, which is particularly noticeable in the house at night.

Start with a pot of one of the species and keep it just moderately moist using a high phosphate—potash fertilizer. If you have to move the plant to larger quarters, make up a Lean Mix with double the quantity of lime in the form of lime chips. Pack the roots hard, tamping down the medium, for these plants grow in dry hills and like close quarters for their roots. Give them the best window or sun porch light you have. Small plants will grow in the light garden too but must be trimmed to keep them within bounds. Cuttings of young wood will root in moist vermiculite.

The principal three species are *C. ladaniferus* with gummy foliage and white flowers with a red center and many golden anthers, *C. laurifolius* with similar flowers, and *C. purpureus* with pink flowers and a purple center.

Citrus. Orange. Lemon. Kumquat. ***Rutaceae.*** Asia. Perennial. Fragrance, essential oils, and medicinal.

The citrus plants have been used everywhere for their fruit, their flavoring oils, their sweet scent, as a refreshing drink and a source of vitamins. For indoor herbalists it matters little whether one or another of the species or cultivars is recommended as long as it is a good plant in the house. Fortunately there are a number that belong in any exotic herb garden. Chief of these are:

Citrus fortunella. Kumquat. There are several dwarf bushy varieties that bloom and fruit easily.

Citrus limonia Meyeri. Meyer's Lemon is a famous old houseplant.

Citrus mitis, the Calamondin Orange. These are little bushes with white fragrant flowers and small bright orange fruits. In New York these can be seen growing, blooming, and fruiting in all kinds of store windows, proof positive that it performs.

Citrus taitensis, the Otaheite Orange. A somewhat larger, bushy houseplant.

There are others of course, including the big-fruited ponderosas. But don't fool around with orange and lemon pits. The seeds often harbor scale and other insects, and these special varieties are so much better as flower and fruit producers.

Citrus plants like an ordinary soil that is somewhat on the acid side. Rich Mix with one part of baked-clay cat litter (Hartz Mountain) added makes a good medium for them. Fertilize with high nitrate formulas. These plants grow well but slowly and take a couple of years to reach bearing size. Plants from nurseries and florist shops are usually ready to bloom. Keep just moderately moist. Direct or bright indirect sunlight part of the day is needed to bring on the clean-smelling sweet white flowers and the bright fruits.

Too often citrus trees are just an untidy mass of foliage, with leaves or fruit saving them from pure ugliness. Good trimming can make a beautiful object from these ugly ducklings. They can be dwarfed, trained into a long cane which is bent to make a circle, trimmed to a conical form, and so forth. In the house such a plant is no longer just an object but becomes a work of art. Citrus are among the easiest and most satisfactory of houseplants and should receive special treatment to make them an aesthetic experience. They will grow nicely under fluorescent light if you keep them within bounds.

The variety of shrubby *Clerodendron* most in cultivation is *C. fragrans flore-pleno*, with masses of double flowers.

Clerodendron fragrans. Glory Bower. **Verbenaceae.** China, Japan. Perennial. Fragrant flowers.

The genus *Clerodendron* includes a considerable number of bushes and vines which are exceedingly beautiful and a few which are fragrant. They are quite popular in California and Florida gardens and are grown in greenhouses in the north. They are excellent subjects for indoor growing because, in spite of the large size to which they can grow in nature, they can be pruned and trained to very manageable dimensions.

    C. fragrans has big masses of pink flowers which are very fragrant. *C. trichotomum* deserves more the label of herb since the leaves are also fragrant. The white flowers have a reddish calyx. *C. concinna*, which has pink flowers, grows only fifteen inches high. *C. glabrum* is white flowered and has fruity aromatic foliage. *C. bungei* and *C. ugandens* have bright blue flowers.

    All of these plants are available from exotic nurseries, and seed is also offered by a few. Seeds take a few weeks to germinate. Culture is quite simple except for the necessity of trimming the larger shrubs to keep them within bounds—unless you have a sun porch with plenty of space and light. They are all evergreen.

    We recommend trying to keep these plants in a 6-inch pot and growing them for their fine appearance as foliage plants and their

110

aromatic leaves. If you get flowers, that's the bonus. They require Rich Mix and plenty of watering during active growth, a humidity of 50 percent or better and a minimum of 60° F. They are strong-growing plants and give little trouble. If they get mites, just wash off the leaves thoroughly every week for a while.

Still another plant must be mentioned although all efforts to include it as a herb are in vain. That is the great vine *Clerodendron thomsoniae.* It is a strong grower that will climb to the roof of a greenhouse and spread far and wide. But the indoor grower can keep it short and shrubby in a 4-to-6-inch pot. The long-lasting clusters of flowers have pure white calyxes and blood red exserted corollas. It is one of the most startling and beautiful phenomena of the plant world. Grow this vine just like the other clerodendrons with one exception. Whenever the flowers dry up and no more buds appear, withdraw water entirely and let the plant lose its leaves. Then keep it dry for about a month. In summer because of the heat and dryness it is advisable to give the roots a very small amount of water once a week but in winter this is unnecessary. At the end of the month increase watering slowly and the plant will green out and set buds immediately.

Clitoria ternatea. Butterfly Pea. **Leguminosae.** India. Perennial vine. Medicinal.

What a pleasure that, having freed ourselves from the narrow confines of a European traditional herb garden, we can grow the butterfly pea indoors as a legitimate medicinal herb. Indeed, we would have to acquire a larger number of ailments to do justice to such a versatile simple. In its home country it is used for the relief of earache, for swollen glands, and for ulcers. More, it is a powerful purgative (the roots) and treatment for enlargement of the abdominal viscera. The roasted powdered seeds are given to children suffering from colic and constipation plus weakness of sight, sore throat, mucous disorders, and skin diseases. And if you are bit by a cobra, take one or two ounces.

It's a herb all right and, in addition, a beautiful small vine with very large "electric" blue flowers. Among its merits is its tolerance of trimming, which allows you to keep it as a small shrub in the window or under lights.

Plant the seeds in your propagation box to a depth of two or three times their diameter. They will come up in fifteen to twenty-five days. As the seeds are pretty large, the seedlings can be transplanted to a pot as soon as they have leaves. A 4- or 5-incher for a single plant is adequate. Use Lean Mix with lime and keep just moist. A temperature of 65° F or higher will induce flowers. Place the plant on the side of the window, where it can follow a trellis, or keep it trimmed to a shrub under lights. Fertilize very sparingly with high nitrate solution. Since this is a twiner it can be trained up a dowel or stake. The flowers easily set seed and lengths of vine can be rooted.

The seed or bean that produces our breakfast refresher (coffee) grows into a fine shrub with shiny, very quilted leaves. The plant blooms very easily under artificial light. This is a much shapelier and handsomer plant than many of the popular tropical foliage plants with uniformly large leaves.

Coffea arabica. Coffee. ***Rubiaceae.*** Tropical Africa. Perennial. Medicinal and aromatic. Fragrant flowers.

We may have doubts about some herbal medicines but there is no question that the roasted seeds of *Coffea arabica,* brewed by various methods, make a beverage that is both aromatic and medicinal. It is the first medicine we take each morning, it exhales an aroma which is pure ambrosia, and imbibing it prevents us from collapsing at the breakfast table. You can grow your own tree either from a plant or from the bean. Seedsmen have the seed, but, if you know a friendly coffee grinder, you can get a few whole green seeds. The plants can be had, quite small, from most garden centers and exotic florists.

There are quite a few varieties of the coffee plant, with leaves varying from quilted oval ones to rather pointy types. The flowers are small, white, and very fragrant. You will have flowers but not the bean.

These are easy plants to grow as small or medium-size shrubs as they take to pruning. Use our Rich Mix and move the plant according to its needs or your intentions to larger pots; eventually you can have a tub if the space is available. But a plant no more than eight inches high, if properly pruned and cultured, will produce bloom under lights or in a window. Fertilize heavily with high nitrate formula. Humidity is not an important factor but bloom is more likely at over 50 percent and at temperatures above 65°—that is for most of the plants we have had. There are upland types of coffee tree which do best in the 50° to 65° range. However, most of those sold in nurseries are the warmer types.

What an oddly shaped plant is samphire. If it were not for its herbal use, we would never think of growing such a humble plant in the house. Out of doors it looks like nothing at all. But in the home herb garden it displays a symmetrical pattern that is most unusual among cultivated plants.

Crithmum maritimum. Samphire. ***Umbelliferae.*** Europe. Perennial. Culinary.

We are attracted to crithmum by its name, samphire, a rather fine-sounding title for the humblest of plants. The English, who are to say the least capricious about food, neglect some very good things and go for oddities like nettles and samphire. The latter is a seashore weed which, it must be admitted, looks more amusing in a pot than on the ground. From a single stem a rosette of fleshy branches arches out, each equipped with a few fleshy leaves that are grey green and opposite. The effect is strangely airy—in a pot. These branches are cut for inclusion in salad and are said to be tasty. Our one plant is too small for the experiment, which might kill it.

It is, however, very easy to grow as long as it is given Spartan treatment. In nature it lives off almost nothing—a Thoreau sort of plant —and therefore you must treat it the same. Give it Succulent Mix, moisture, and sun. Once a month, fertilize with anything available. A young plant will grow and need a bigger pot but we intend not to go over a 4-incher. We figure it can starve flourishingly in the small space. However, if you become addicted, it can be moved if you are careful not to disturb the earth ball more than necessary. Branches with leaves will put forth roots in moist vermiculite and, if the plant gets large, it can be simply divided at root level.

Daphne odora. Thymelaeaceae. China, Japan. Perennial. Fragrant flowers.

This shrub is so commonly grown in the South and so well liked that it is surprising we have not brought it indoors. It attains about four feet, is evergreen, has 3-inch shiny leaves and clusters of very fragrant white or purplish flowers. Try it in the house in a small tub, in Rich Mix without lime, and fertilize with high nitrate formula. Keep moderately moist and give good light in early spring. With careful pruning, this daphne can be accommodated by a much smaller pot and can make it in a window or even under the lights.

Drosera rotundifolia. Sundew. ***Sarraceniaceae.*** United States. Perennial. Medicinal.

Oh, what a boon to man is this little carnivorous plant, whose leaves, covered with hairs tipped by a sticky fluid, trap tiny insects. According to Leyel it's great for all throat and lung conditions, successful with arteriosclerosis and high blood pressure ("but the patient often finds it very fatiguing in its effect"), and is said to cure tubercular glands and hip joint pains. Wow.

You can buy these flat rosettes from wild flower nurseries and dealers in exotic and carnivorous plants. It will grow nicely in just a bed of sphagnum moss in a terrarium along with *Sarracenia purpurea,* the Venus-flytrap, and pinguicula. High humidity, warmth, well-aerated medium (the sphagnum moss), and good light will keep it happy. From time to time it will throw up a scape with pink or white flowers which stay open just to midday. Don't try feeding it flies—it has a very limited appetite and will do all right for itself. Don't fertilize.

Epigaea repens. Trailing Arbutus. ***Ericaceae.*** United States. Perennial. Medicinal and fragrant.

Trailing arbutus will grow more luxuriantly in a cool cellar under fluorescent light than out in the woods. In fact it will do all right in partial shade near a window. It requires very acid soil and should be grown in an azalea pot. Treat your mix with citric acid or aluminum sulphate (Lean Mix) or take a chance on oak woods soil where arbutus grows.

Only nursery-grown plants should be acquired, for this is one of the wild flowers about which the conservationists are most concerned. It is a coarse little plant, growing perfectly flat, rooting as it goes, and having very rough oval leaves. The pinky-white waxy flowers are intensely perfumed. But the plants will not bloom until after being subject to a period of freezing. So put your pot out of doors for a couple of months in the depth of winter and then bring it in again. We haven't tried the refrigerator, though that should work too. However, there is risk that the fridge will be all plants and no food, so try the windowsill instead. The medicinal properties are said to be very similar to those of bearberry.

Epigaea should be kept rather dry during the summer heat. It can take it.

A forbidden plant for digging in the woods, trailing arbutus is an easy and unusual plant for the house. The leaves are as leathery as the flowers are waxy. The scent is fabulous.

Horsetails (*Equisetum*) grow everywhere in the country but are so plain that only a naturalist —or aesthete—will notice them. The spike at the top is the fruiting stalk. When the moisture on the leaves dries off they will spread into a filmy umbrella which is as beautiful as the laciest fern frond.

Equisetum arvense. Horsetail. ***Equisetaceae.*** North America. Perennial. Medicinal.

The idea of growing horsetail indoors is totally bizarre. Nobody raises it in any kind of garden, for it is a common weed of damp ditches and railroad tracks and does not flower. Yet some species would make excellent ground covers in shady, moist places.

It is one of the simplest and most ancient of plants—a relic of the carboniferous age. The fluid extract formerly was considered valuable in the treatment of gonorrhea, dropsy and other urinary problems. It must have done the dinosaurs a world of good.

The low-growing horsetails, of most interest for indoors, look so much alike that unless you take to your botany any one will do. *E. arvense, pratense,* and *sylvaticum* all send up fruiting stems first, followed by branched sterile stems. *E. palustre* and *littorale* have stems all alike. *Sylvaticum* is the prettiest, having the most delicate and spreading branches.

Since there is as yet no conservation problem here and no likelihood that the depredations of indoor growers will become a menace, we can recommend digging up a clump when the fruiting stem appears in the spring. Chances are that you will have enough of the sandy, wet soil it requires for potting. But pick a deep pot and line the bottom with an inch of pebbles before stuffing in the soil. Provide the pot with a saucer and keep that full at all times. Set the pot anywhere with reflected light. The result is more attractive than many other herbs. In winter just put the pot outside the window for about three months. Never fertilize.

115

The pretty pompon flowers and graceful long leaves of the blue gum.

Wow. This is the tree *Eucalyptus globulus* can become. But, we are learning that many of the tropical trees and shrubs can be kept small in the house and make handsome specimens.

Eucalyptus globulus. Blue Gum. ***Myrtaceae.*** Australia. Perennial. Medicinal and aromatic.

The almost innumerable species and varieties of eucalyptus from the Antipodes have been introduced all over the world for ornamental and economic use. *E. globulus*, a giant growing up to 300 feet, is the source of eucalyptus oil, which is a component of cough medicines, inhalants, and many other remedies. It is also recognized as a good foliage houseplant when grown from seed. Dwarf varieties are available from seedsmen. The trunk is greyish bluish and the leaves also have the tint, and the latter are aromatic. Seeds take about four weeks to germinate.

Move from smaller to larger pots trimming to your needs. Eventually it can use a tub. Use Rich Mix, moderate watering, and feed with high nitrate fertilizer. It likes bright reflected light. Ordinary house temperatures are suitable and it is not particular about humidity. With its small leaves, it makes a good bonsai with training.

There are many other eucalyptuses worth trying, among them *E. Gunnii,* with fragrant leaves from which Australian gum is extracted. *E. maculata* var. *citriodora* has lemon-scented leaves.

Far more attractive than an avocado.

Young fennel looks so much like dill that it is hard to tell them apart. And, in fact, they are very closely related. However fennel takes off and grows into a very big plant with a large, white, juicy delicious root. Never try to grow it that big in the house. But as a juvenile it is a graceful plant and the slight licorice flavor of the leaves is pleasant in salads.

Foeniculum vulgare. Fennel. **Umbelliferae.** Europe. Grown as an annual. Culinary.

Fennel is mostly grown in the garden for its heavy white roots which make an excellent vegetable, cooked or raw. The seed is used in pickling and flavoring and the leaves, which are aromatic, are similar to dill in appearance and flavor. However, the slight anise taste is not a great attraction and the plant, being much bigger, is not as good indoors as dill. As a houseplant, it is somewhat like asparagus fern, with its long stems and lacy foliage, so you may want to give it a try.

Seed germinates in about fourteen days, and the seedlings should be potted up in a Lean Mix with lime. From there on give it starvation rations to make it grow slowly and never move it to anything larger than a 4-inch pot. In that way it may stay quite decorative for a long while. As the bulb matures at the base, the regimen can become even more Spartan—little water and no fertilizer. If, in spite of this mistreatment it grows too high, lop off a section of the central stem.

You'll have to get down low to see the waxy bells of the wintergreen hidden under the thickish leaves. Flower and berries have the characteristic odor that turns up in chewing gum as well as medications.

Gaultheria procumbens. Wintergreen. **Ericaceae.** North America. Perennial. Medicinal and aromatic.

Oil of wintergreen is used as a flavorant in candy and pills or drops, and in lotions and unguents, very much like peppermint.

The plant, only a couple of inches high, with a few inch-long leaves, has bell-shaped waxy flowers like huckleberry or bearberry. It moves along by means of underground roots. Put it in a woodland terrarium with very acid soil along with pipsissewa and partridgeberry. The bright red fruits are decorative against the deep greens. Keep moist in partial shade, as cool as possible in summer and don't fertilize.

Gelsemium sempervirens. Carolina Jessamine. ***Loganiaceae.*** Southern
United States. Perennial. Fragrant flowers and medicinal.

This lovely, yellow-flowered vine with the sweet odor grows wild in
moist places of the South. The shape of the blooms is a trumpet 1½
inches long. Because it is as much a small shrub as a vine, it can be kept
from climbing in the house by judicious pruning of new growth, whereupon it will develop a branched rather woody stem, and bloom off and
on throughout the year.

Contrary to so many of our true houseplants from the tropics,
gelsemium requires a very acid soil. Use Rich Mix without lime and, if
need be (leaves turn yellow or it refuses to grow), treat with a citric acid
or aluminum sulphate solution. However, the peat mix is usually acid
enough. Use high nitrate fertilizer and keep moist. For bloom, the
temperature should not go below 65° and a humidity level of 50 percent
or better also helps. Give it reflected light in the window and place it
about six inches beneath your fluorescent tubes. Plants can be bought
from a number of nurseries and it can be propagated from cuttings of
young growth. Seed is also available.

The fluid extract was formerly used for all kinds of disorders. Best
of all, it was claimed, was its ability to "allay nervous excitement and
irritation." What a fine name for a new tranquilizer—Carolina Jessamine!

The yellow trumpets of *Gelsemium* appear on mature plants that are only a few inches
high. Allowed to run, it becomes a vine of modest proportions. In the house, keep it
shrubby and it may bloom all year, especially under lights.

Curry powder is a mixture of Asiatic spices with a characteristic unmistakable odor that it is hard to believe any plant could imitate. This harmless-looking daisy plant with the grey green leaves accomplishes the miracle. Rub the leaves and you are wafted to India. We have seen carefully trimmed and cultured shrubs of the curry plant that were 18 to 24 inches high and perfectly shaped woody shrubs.

Helichrysum angustifolium. Curry Plant. *Compositae.* Mediterranean. Aromatic foliage.

We first learned about this remarkable aromatic plant when a distinguished greenhouse grower displayed a splendidly grown and trimmed specimen at a flower show. We rubbed a leaf by chance—and were shocked to find that it smelled exactly like curry powder. Since real curry powder is compounded of numerous aromatic spices, it is incredible that a leaf could combine the odors of them all.

The helichrysums are called everlastings because they have flowers that retain their color and form when dried. The most popular is the garden strawflower. Some of the other species, like the curry plant, have blooms which are quite tiny. But nobody raises the latter for this purpose indoors or out.

You can start with a plant that will be no more than four inches high, with one-inch-long narrow very woolly leaves. As it branches and grows, keep it well trimmed back so that it branches again. In this way, after a couple of years, you will have a specimen that is a solid twiggy ball or mushroom of soft grey leaves with that wonderful aroma.

Helichrysum needs your best window or fluorescent light, Lean Mix with lime, and hardly any fertilizing until the plant becomes larger. We fertilize with a mild solution of 20–20–20 at every watering. Keep it in small pots. Eventually it may develop a thick trunk and require a small tub. Temperatures down to 40° are fine and it tolerates dry air. It is a slow grower, like some of the prostrate rosemaries and should be treated much the same.

A black-and-white photograph hardly does justice to the beauty of *Humea* with its contrasting large foliage and delicate spikes of pendent flowers.

Humea elegans. Compositae. Australia. Biennial. Fragrance of leaves.

This is a handsome 6-foot shrub with large wrinkled sweet-scented leaves, and flowers in panicles, red, rose, or pink.

Worth growing for the foliage alone, this is a plant that prefers warm temperatures, ample watering, and feeding. Use Rich Mix without lime and fertilize with full-strength nitrate solutions. The plants should be kept a little dryer in winter. Seed is available and germinates promptly. Grow in a ten-inch pot.

This is the showiest variety of jasmine, *Jasminum sambac,* 'Grand Duke.' Fully double, the pure white flowers are deliciously perfumed.

Jasminum. Jasmine. ***Oleaceae.*** China and India. Perennial. Flower fragrance.

The superiority of indoor growing over outdoor is nowhere more clearly demonstrated than with the jasmines. Due to fluorescent light, humidifiers, and our warm home temperatures, we can enjoy the wonderful scent of these tropical plants in flower anywhere in the house.

The jasmines are vines which can be kept as small shrubs by drastic pruning. We find this is generally true of the woodier vines, while those that are very juicy stemmed grow too fast and resent dwarfing. They want Rich Mix, lime, the highest humidity you can give them, temperatures over 65° and good but not necessarily direct sunlight. Give light fertilizing with a balanced formula. These requirements are typically tropical when bloom is desired and have only become possible in the house in recent years.

The easiest, and one of the loveliest of the jasmines, is the Arabian jasmine, *Jasminum sambac* with two varieties, 'Maid of Orleans' with single flowers and 'Grand Duke' with double ones. The single flowers are like pinwheels, while the doubles look like small gardenias.

Another beautiful jasmine is *J. gracile magnificum,* with long oval pointed leaves and flat flowers with seven or eight flat white petals. Others are *J. mesnyi* (sold as primulinum) and, with larger flowers and broader petals, *J. officinale,* poet's jasmine. *J. humile* has yellow flowers.

All of these are wonderfully fragrant. Be patient with your jasmine plant. It will require time to get used to you but then will always be in flower. Also, keep that humidity up.

Our favorite lavender is *dentata*. The other lavenders might be mistaken for other herbs but *dentata* is unmistakable. And whereas most lavenders have very little odor in the house, *dentata* needs only be brushed with the hand to emit its sweet soapy aroma. Being tender, it also behaves far better than the others indoors.

Lavandula. Lavender. ***Labiatae.*** Europe. Perennial. Fragrance.

The lavenders offer an important lesson on the difference between outdoor and indoor growing, especially in respect to choosing the right varieties for best results. There is considerable variation in the species and any number of hybrids. But our main consideration in making our choice is whether they are hardy perennials or not. If they are, they go dormant in winter in the house and require cold to revive them. The English herb gardens and nurseries have selected strains which do well in the island climate and for that very reason do not do well for us. American gardeners have selected the hardiest of the English strains because our winters are even more severe than theirs. For this reason the attempt to grow the great English lavenders—Munstead and Hidcote strains, for instance—is not impossible indoors but far less satisfactory than concentrating on plants from the Mediterranean which prefer our warm house temperatures. As a matter of record we found on trial that these northern lavenders were not only difficult to grow in the house but developed very little fragrance indoors.

Then a friend (Evelyn Cronin of Wellesley Hills, Massachusetts) gave us a pot of *Lavandula dentata*. Whereas the other lavenders have simple leaves, *L. dentata* has very odd ones that are narrow, long, and scalloped. The appearance of the plant is far more attractive, and just brushing against it brings out clouds of the soft sweet odor. It grows, with a little pruning, in a very bushy manner and sends up in summer long stalks bearing a short spike of closely packed white flowers. Because it is also a much easier plant to grow indoors than the others, we find that, until we have experience with more of the southern-grown plants, that this is the only one about which we can become enthusiastic as a houseplant.

Buy a small plant and repot it in Rich Mix with lime chips. The trick with this plant is to keep it fairly dry without desiccating it. *Dentata* definitely does not like to be soaked—so let it really dry out a bit between waterings. Nevertheless it is a very thirsty plant on hot summer days and has to be watched to prevent real drying out. Another point —it is a plant that dislikes crowding. Give it a bit of air space.

Set *L. dentata* in partial sun in a window or any position under the lights. Fertilize with a balanced formula. Normal house temperatures are satisfactory summer and winter. A 4-inch pot is the maximum you will need.

The same culture applies to two other southern lavenders which, in our opinion, are less attractive.

L. pedunculata is a small shrub with greyish green leaves and violet flower spikes on long stalks.

L. stoechas has purple black flowers and greyish leaves. Like many other lavenders the leaves are very narrow and plain in outline. Given a chance it will grow to three feet.

All the lavenders propagate easily from cuttings.

Lippia citriodora. Lemon Verbena. ***Verbenaceae.*** Argentina and Chile. Perennial. Culinary and fragrant-leaved.

The true lemon verbena leaves when rubbed give forth an odor that is not so much that of the lemon fruit as of sweet candy lemon drops. The similarity is perfect. In English herbals the plant is always listed as deciduous but this is not true in the house and it proves of very easy culture. The light green leaves, about 1½ inches long, are pointed at either end and have even ribbing at right angles to the midvein. The leaves can be dried and used as an aromatic and flavoring herb in cooking.

It is best to purchase a small plant and take cuttings from it. The three leading nodes of a branch will set roots in a couple of weeks in a propagating box. The parent plant, no matter how much trimmed, turns woody after a year, and greenery will be confined to the tips of the branches. The effect is rather oriental and quite pretty. When well pruned it can become a respectable bonsai. However, always keep a few young plants on the way if you want to maintain them in 4-inch pots.

Lemon verbena does well under lights or in the reflected light of a window, in Lean Mix with lime, and watered moderately. Don't dry out completely. Use a balanced fertilizer.

L. canescens (repens), a ground cover of the West Coast, is a lovely creeping plant with lilac flowers in small clusters. *L. ligustrina* is a southern small shrub with fragrant white flowers.

Lemon verbena looks reasonably neat and compact when small.

Older plants of lemon verbena almost always look like this. We have seen some pretty big ones. The long, squiggly branching is so wild that it becomes decorative with time. For this reason, we often lct lemon verbena run.

The true marjoram.

Majorana hortensis. Sweet Marjoram. **Labiatae.** Europe. Perennial. Culinary.

As a culinary herb marjoram stands between thyme and oregano, being less intense than the latter and sweeter than the former. The typical marjoram must have that slight sweetness in the odor that the other two lack. We bring this up because marjoram and oregano are very closely related and, even in the botanies, the genus name *Majorana* is usually followed by the genus name *Origanum,* in parentheses.

Except in herb and spice mixtures for stuffing chicken and turkey, marjoram is very little used in American kitchens. In our opinion it is as universal as thyme or basil, and we make it part of the "bouquet" for salad dressings and meat dishes of all kinds.

The true sweet marjoram—*Majorana hortensis (Origanum majorana)* —is grown in outdoor herb gardens as an annual. This is only because it is a tender plant. In fact it is perfectly perennial in warmer climates and indoors. The stems are woody and the leaves woolly, rounded, and stalked.

A somewhat stronger flavored marjoram is *Majorana onites (Origanum onites),* also known as French marjoram. It is rather closer in flavor to oregano, is a bigger plant than sweet marjoram, and its leaves are not stalked.

The marjorams should be potted small in Lean Mix with lime and watered sparingly. Use a balanced fertilizer solution. The better the light the better they do. But if you do not mind some straggle, they will tolerate an east window or the ends of the tubes. Trim them for bushiness or develop the tree effect of woody long stems.

126

Marrubium vulgare. Horehound. *Labiatae.* Europe and Asia. Perennial. Medicinal.

A principle of the old medicine was that its effectiveness could be measured by its nasty taste. Horehound drops used to be a sovereign specific for coughs, and we always found them as revolting in flavor as could be desired. The plant grows to three feet in height outdoors and develops branches which bear, like so many labiates, a circle of tiny flowers at the level of the axils. The leaves have an oily, pungent odor which some may find attractive.

Like so many other herbs of Europe, this is pure weed and requires rather poor, lean soil but plenty of watering. By keeping it in a 2½-inch pot, or 4 inches at most, it will look quite handsome. Plant in Lean Mix.

This is another starve-and-enjoy plant for the home herb garden. The leaves will contribute a properly hospital smell with which to compare your more civilized fragrances. Grow from seed, which germinates easily, and thereafter from cuttings.

Cut and cut again, horehound's leaves become reduced in size. With a bit of proportioning this coarse weedy plant will become an ornament of the herb garden. Flies love the herbs (most of them) and cluster around when we photograph them with the windows open.

Lemon balm branching after having been severely cut back. This is how it looks best in the house.

Melissa officinalis. Lemon Balm. ***Labiatae.*** Europe. Perennial. Medicinal and flavorant.

So many of the mints have the same kinds of leaves—shield-shaped, serrated along the edges and rough-stiff hairy. All are somewhat aromatic, some more than others. Melissa is of this type but unique in its strong lemon flavor and odor. The small whitish flowers grow, typically, in clusters in the axils.

Seed, contrary to outdoors, can be planted any time of year, and the seeds will germinate in three to four weeks. A rather strong-growing plant it will reach two feet if not cut often. Therefore the idea is to keep it well trimmed and shapely. It is best to keep it in a four-inch pot in Rich Mix without lime and quite moist. Drying out produces yellow leaves. Give it your best light position.

Outdoors here melissa must be grown as an annual—another advantage for the indoor grower. Propagation is easy by means of cuttings.

This is how lemon balm grows in the wild where it has been naturalized from Europe. When stems and leaves are not cut, it blooms on
tallish stems but it is not much of a show.

So close in appearance to Eau de Cologne mint, this plant possessed a strong orange flavor.

A real teddy bear of a mint with a nice aroma which may remind you of apple or something else. This is *M. rotundifolia*.

Eau de Cologne mint. The odor of the rubbed leaves is one of the most surprising and enjoyable of all the herbs.

Mentha. Mint. ***Labiatae.*** Europe and Asia. Perennial. Culinary, fragrant leaves, and medicinal.

We have before, and could easily here, write an extended essay on the mints which are the most typical of herbs, being useful in all the basic ways and extremely varied due to minor or major differences in habit, leaf shape, odor, and flavor. But a lengthy analysis would be of little practical use to the indoor grower. Our best course is to describe the plant and its culture, list some of the types and leave you to your own devices.

For the outdoor garden these are not disciplined plants chosen for formal settings. Although a few grow tall and straight, they were never handsome plants, their flowering is dull lavender or whitish, and leaves are not very attractive. We grow them, therefore, because of their intense, refreshing aromas and their many uses, rather than as ornamentals.

One reason for their unsuitability in garden designs is their way of propagating themselves by means of their roots—a method that has banished many a more handsome weed from gardens. Mints have relatively shallow roots that travel outward in all directions until they are far enough from the parent to establish their independence. Then they send up stalks above the soil. So a mint plant will break out almost anywhere and, if you want to eradicate it, you must dig up not only what you see above but also what is growing below ground level.

Secondly, the trailing varieties send out long suckers aboveground, with long internodes on the stalks and smaller leaves. These bend down of their own weight and root themselves in the ground. So mints are always on the move above and below ground. We suppose they do this partly because they quickly exhaust the nutritive content of the soil and seek out fairer ground.

These two habits of growth are why we also have problems keeping them in pots for long. They are always trying to get out of them in one way or another and show their displeasure, when they are inhibited, by producing smaller leaves, more suckers, and less aromatic or tasty leaves. Nobody raises a mint as an ornamental.

Having said this, we have to note that anyone interested in herbs for the kitchen is not going to do without the mints and, therefore, we must carry on as best we can.

On the plus side, the mints can be grown in partial shade and will receive at window or under lights plenty of illumination for their needs. Also they present no problems in regard to watering, since it is wet all the way. If they have special needs in regard to fertilizer, we have not discovered them. We use high nitrate fertilizer and hope that this is the best. We have noticed no difference in growth no matter what we use.

As for soil, we use Rich Mix and pot them in shallow containers with as much surface space as we can afford. Then we pin down suckers with hairpins to fill up the empty soil spaces and produce a fair quantity of leaf and a somewhat bushy appearance. Excess suckers are cut off as they appear. Cutting off parts of the good stems for the leaves encourages the suckers and we find that it takes patience to get back good leaf coverage. So we must constantly fuss with them. In the end they get tired of the pot, sulk, and have to be given a new pot and new soil before they will budge again. They are subject to mites, and sometimes aphids, which can be washed off every few days and will disappear.

In the wild, spearmint looks nothing like this, being rather straight stalked and tall. This plant has been pruned to make a far more attractive, and long-lasting, shrub.

Of all the mints, the sharpest and most pepperminty is Corsican mint, the tiniest. In a pot it looks almost like a moss But brush the leaves and the intense, pure odor rises from the little plant. It is said that the original crème de menthe was made from its leaves. Certainly the current insipid product is not.

Betty's mint. Our own maverick mint. It has an undertone of pure peppermint but is less sharp and above it floats a marvelous fruity sweetness. Possibly a hybrid of Eau de Cologne mint and peppermint. House culture has reduced the size of leaves.

In return for your trouble you get wonderful scents and useful dried or fresh leaves for the kitchen.

The principal mints are:

M. aquatica. Water mint. Bergamot mint.

M. citrata. Orange mint. Eau de Cologne mint.

M. crispa. Curly mint.

M. piperita. Peppermint.

M. pulegium. True pennyroyal.

M. requienii. Corsican mint.

M. rotundifolia. Apple mint.

M. spicata. Spearmint.

Spearmint is perhaps the easiest to grow and is certainly the most popular. It has a flavor we find cloying even in a mint julep, in sauce for lamb, and in jellies. It is an erect plant that can be kept trimmed to a moderately bushy growth, and it will not wander as much as some of the others.

Peppermint is our all-around favorite. It has such a clean, fresh flavor and, divorced from sugar, makes a marvelous herb in salads and sauces. Near Eastern cooks know how to use it and it is one of their favorites. Of course peppermint candy is a staple. *M. aquatica* is quite similar.

But for sheer peppermint sharpness there is nothing to match *M. requienii*, the Corsican mint. It is a love of a plant, so tiny that many mosses are larger. In a pot it grows evenly, spreading over the whole surface and completely blanketing it with little leaves. It is said that the original crème de menthe was made with it. The wretched product

The true European pennyroyal is no great shakes as a plant and hardly comparable with the better mints for flavor.

Hedeoma pulegoides—American pennyroyal—is neither a particularly good mint nor an especially attractive plant. There are dozens of wild members of the mint family which are similar. But for the collector of herbal Americana it's a must.

usually sold under that name certainly bears no faintest resemblance in flavor to this marvelous little herb. Corsican mint is fun to raise in a terrarium, alone or in a small pot as part of large planting. For those who like the miniatures this is a gem.

Curly mint is coarse and quilted. We see it often in the market where a taste of a leaf reveals very little flavor.

Apple mint has a sweet, rather indefinite aroma but is the most ornamental of the group. Leaves are quite large, oval to round, thickish soft and whitish furry. Stems are thick and the plant can be trimmed to maintain a quite handsome set of symmetrical overlapping concentric leaves.

There are numerous fine variations among the mints. Thus *Mentha citrata* is, according to some, both orange mint and Eau de Cologne mint. However, in practice orange mint smells very strongly of orange, which is a bit of a switch, since the herbs so often tend to have a lemony odor. Eau de Cologne mint, on the other hand, really smells like the old-fashioned perfume rather than modern imitations. It is the unique perfume among the mints. Both of these mints have rather shiny foliage. *M. citrata* is somewhat pointy while Eau de Cologne is more rounded and the surface is very oily in appearance.

Finally, we must mention Betty's mint. It is one of the many hybrids of this shamelessly interbreeding genus. Betty brought us a sprig and we coveted the plant and have had it growing ever since. We wave it in the air whenever we pass it and its cool fragrance is a delight. It is minty but perfumed—more minty than Eau de Cologne and also more intense. Perhaps it is a hybrid of Eau de Cologne and peppermint. The leaves are quite smooth. Not all hybrids are as good. If you buy at a nursery, you may run across such maverick mints, which are worth collecting.

The pennyroyals are hardly worth mentioning except for those who wish to collect mints. The true pennyroyal is a bitter-flavored herb, and *Hedeoma pulegioides*, the American or false pennyroyal, is no better.

Micromeria. Labiatae. Mostly Europe. Perennial. Aromatic.

Micromeria looks much like and is grown like the thymes. *M. corsica* is an evergreen shrub 3 to 6 inches high and *M. piperella* grows to 6 inches. Both have thymelike flowers and odd medicinal odors which attract cats. So treat your cat and have a nice easy little pot of herb for it to munch. They like sun and warmth, with ordinary soil.

    M. chamissonis is called Yerba Buena and comes from California. It has long rooting stems and white flowers.

Mitchella repens. Partridgeberry. *Rubiaceae.* United States. Perennial. Medicinal.

The red berries of partridgeberry are those you usually see in woodland terrariums. It grows beautifully along with pipsissewa, wintergreen, et al. Very acid soil and moss, coolth, moisture but not sogginess, and no fertilizer are the recommendations for a healthy plant. Very little window or fluorescent light is needed although this, and the other plants, will grow better if medium bright light can be provided without raising the temperature above 80° in summer. The Indians used the diluted extract of partridgeberry as a tonic.

Mustard and cress ready for shearing. It makes wonderful peppery sandwiches. *Left* mustard, *right* cress.

Mustard and Cress. **Brassica alba** and **Lepidium sativum. Cruciferae.** Europe. Annual. Flavor.

We depart from our usual heading because of the inseparability of these two plants. If they are not familiar to you, you will be delighted to make their acquaintance. In England mustard and cress sandwiches are as much a staple as the hot dog in America. And this is one crop you can gather fast and often.

We have bought our seeds in England. They come in large packs because the seed is fairly large and also because very many are used at a single planting. This is how you do it.

Best for planting is a baked clay saucer, though any shallow pot will do. Figure on a diameter of at least 4 inches. If you start to become an addict you will need more and more space.

Fill the container to near the top with Lean Mix that is thoroughly moistened. Strew half the surface with cress so that almost the whole area is completely covered. Sprinkle a thin coat of additional mix over the seeds. Set the container in a window or under lights and wait four days. By that time the cress will be up.

Now plant the mustard seed in the same way on the other half. In forty-eight hours that will be up.

Two to three days later your plants will be an inch or more high and a solid lawn of mustard and cress. Take long scissors and cut all of it right down to the ground, avoiding getting dirt mixed in with the herb.

Make a bread and butter sandwich spreading the combined herbs in between. Eat and enjoy. Then start a new crop. Fun and delicious food for all ages. You will never again want to be without mustard and cress.

There are many forms of myrtle but this is the original *Myrtus communis,* the ancient herb with classic overtones. Its principal merit is that it can be trained into rather good-sized leafy shrubs. The leaves are slightly fragrant and little white flowers may appear at any time of year.

Myrtus communis. Myrtle. ***Myrtaceae.*** Southern Europe. Perennial. Aromatic and medicinal.

The myrtle is widely grown in herb gardens, mainly for its small leaves and neat form which can be clipped and trained. The leaves give out, when crushed, an odd combination of lemon and medicinal fragrances. Its popularity is due to biblical relationships and its being very holy to the Romans. In medicine it is said to "check night sweats of phthisis." Never having had phthisis, we cannot vouch for it.

Nevertheless myrtle is a pleasant little plant with opposite dark green shiny leaves on wandlike stems which are relatively short and become woody with time. It *can* grow up to 10 feet but very slowly and is best kept in small pots. There are any number of forms—compact varieties, very small-leaved ones, and variegations. Flowers are white and fruit black.

Grow myrtle in Rich Mix and keep moderately moist. Fertilize little with high nitrate formula. It is tolerant of low light conditions, so reflected light near the window, or 12 inches under the lights, will do.

Myrtle should be even more popular indoors than out, for it is one of those plants that can be kept to any size and trained to any shape so that the aesthetics are up to you.

Variegated myrtle looks very much like a number of other variegated shrubby plants. Here it had developed a central stem long enough to provide a good piece for the cutting box.

First results of our first pruning of a variegated myrtle. The lower branches are beginning to grow. Soon we can nip the tips of the top branches and force further thickening of the leafy growth.

We grow catnip as a curiosity and because we do not have cats. Many cat lovers, it seems, disapprove of sending their pets on a "trip." This is a much bigger, coarser plant than *Nepeta mussini* and the flowering is rather messy.

Nepeta mussini is far more popular as a garden plant than the better-known catnip. Also it grows much smaller and is easy to maintain in a pot. Being rather tender, it stays green all winter in the house but should be pruned in spring to produce new clothes. Because of grey leaves and pink flowers it can be attractive when well grown.

Nepeta mussini. Nepeta cataria. Catnip. **Labiatae.** Europe. Perennial. Medicinal.

Nepeta mussini is a pleasant small minty plant with attractive foliage and quite bright dark pink flowers. *Nepeta cataria* is theoretically the more interesting plant. It is a big coarse thing, woolly, with clumpy spikes of white flowers. In fact it belongs to a whole tribe of quite unattractive, weedy members of the mint family, and it has never been used for anything but the befuddling of cats. So, in practice, unless you have a cat, there is no earthly reason why you should attempt to grow it. If you do, just handle it like spearmint.

As for *Nepeta mussini*—at least it does not sprawl like most of the mints grown in the house. Pot it in Lean Mix with lime and place it in good light. Keep it moderately moist and fertilize regularly with 20–20–20 solution and you will have a respectable-looking plant which may bloom for a short period. As you can see, we are not enthusiastic—considering the other choices. But, then, you may love it.

139

Our wonderful French basil.

Ocimum basilicum. Basil. ***Labiatae.*** Tropical Asia. Annual. Culinary.

The king of culinary herbs, as its name indicates, basil is one of the essential ingredients of a bouquet garni and has infinite uses in the kitchen. The leaves are wonderful in salad and have an affinity for tomatoes. The dried leaves are best for poultry dressing.

Typical of the chief herbs, this one has an infinite number of variations, the differences among them being so great that one might suspect them of being different species. All one can say is that the stalk is juicy, the leaves plentiful, the latter shiny and green or purple, and the size varies according to the strain. In England and here outdoors it is grown as an annual. Indoors its life-span is affected not by weather but its tendency to become woody with age and produce fewer leaves. The white flowers are charming—growing in little circlets around the spike.

The outdoor varieties tend to be as large as possible. The popular 'Dark Opal' strain, for instance, may have 4-inch leaves. This is so that the user can get a large quick crop from a few plants. But they are out of proportion in the house. The bush basil, called *Ocimum minimum,* is just a smaller variety with quite tiny leaves. It is the best for pot culture if one is stuck with American seeds.

Far better is seed we have had from Vilmorin, the Burpee of France. The plant has small light green leaves aplenty, branches profusely after cutting, and is far better flavored than other types we have tried. Seed planted on November 3 was up on the seventh and transplanted on December 11. Cuttings root in a week to ten days. So once you have a couple of plants you can have as many as you wish very quickly.

We grow these plants in 2½-inch pots in Rich Mix with plenty of lime and, contrary to the advice in some books, keep them wet all the time. We use any fertilizer which is handy. As far as light is concerned the plants seem to do well under the best light and at quite a distance —for instance a good foot—from the tubes and well to the side of a window. In our opinion this is the most simple of the herbs to grow. A few pots take good care of our actual kitchen needs. The plants are very handsome when neatly trimmed. Other European seed firms have good basils of this type but none quite like Vilmorin's.

There are also lemon-scented basils of which we have plants, the original seed having been collected in Luxor, Egypt, by a friend. The appearance is almost the same as our French basil except that the leaves are somewhat more toothed.

Although these particular seeds are not easily available you might find interesting basils by trying different seedsmen. Faute de mieux almost any seed offered will grow easily in the house. Basil is just that versatile.

Our Egyptian lemon basil. Just one of many rooted cuttings.

Golden creeping oregano. Possibly so-called *Origanum aureum*. Not a particularly good culinary plant, the leaves are pleasantly aromatic and growth is compact. The leaf shape is particularly interesting.

Origanum. Oregano. ***Labiatae.*** Europe. Perennial. Culinary and medicinal.

The *Origanum-Majorana* complex is complex indeed. Even with botany in hand, several herbals, and lots of illustrations and plants, it is impossible to decide just where one begins and the other ends. Flavorwise, culinary marjoram seems to be a mild oregano, and oregano, which is much stronger flavored, seems to verge into, of all things, thyme. If we were to follow the botanical listings of origanums we would end up with marjorams and vice versa. Yet at any well-stocked herb nursery, there are always several forms of both on display. So we might call this The Search for the True Oregano. Chances are the two herbs have been so intermingled by natural garden hybridization that the plants we know are all first-class illegitimates except for a few specially grown strains— which happen to be hardy, English, and not too suitable for indoor growing.

The confusion is further indicated by personal experience. We had never grown oregano and asked for a pot at a well-known herb nursery where we received more than the usual customer attention. We were handed a plant which we bought on the spot. At home we tried the leaves over and over again but found none of the true oregano pungency. So we planted some marjoram seed and, sure enough, as soon as they came up we knew that our plant was marjoram.

We suspect that had we asked for marjoram at the nursery we would have been given the same plant. And it is possible that the underlying problem is habit rather than ignorance. The English have never been attracted to the true oregano flavor in their food and look upon it as something associated with the inferior tomato sauces of southern Italy. Hence oregano becomes a mere name for marjoram. On another occasion we found a nursery selling an "oregano" that was as tasteless as any nonculinary weed of the mint family.

142

Described as tender oregano—meaning not winter hardy. So much better for the house. Growth is compact and attractive. The leaves have a taste and odor between that of dried marjoram and dried oregano. Many similar types will be found at a well-stocked herb nursery. Pick them for their appearance and "tenderness," which means that they do not require a winter freeze and remain evergreen.

Italian oregano. The herb nurseryman had received this plant from Italy without a botanical name. But, contrary to some of the "oreganos" we have tested, this one has the real odor and flavor. When buying plants for culinary use in the oregano-marjoram complex judge by smell and taste—not by the label.

Cuban oregano is really *Coleus amboinensis*—not a true oregano at all. It has been introduced recently from the Islands where it is popular as a culinary herb. The leafy growth habit is attractive.

Oreganos seem to be, as far as the indoor gardener is concerned, several varieties of plants with upright or somewhat sprawling stems and small heart-shaped, hairy, usually rather greyish, leaves. If the plant has a strong oregano odor and taste, that is all we really have to know as far as the kitchen is concerned. The other question is which one is best for growing in the house.

Of all the oreganos for display the dittany of Crete is our favorite. We have treated it separately because it is recognized as quite a different plant from the others. Our second choice has no name. We bought it from a nurseryman who reported receiving it from a traveling friend as Italian oregano. We have illustrated it and all we can say is that it conforms to the right flavor.

Among the named origanums are *O. microphyllum,* with very small leaves, and *O. aureum,* a low, not very attractive, yellowish-leaved plant. Our only advice is that you look around at nurseries for oreganos and buy by nose and taste—not appearance. At least the senses should take priority.

In the house these are small plants to be kept in small pots. Or try three or more plants of different varieties in a shallow hanging basket and let them trail over the side. They like a Lean Mix with plenty of lime chips, as much sun as you can give them, and very moderate watering. Let them dry out a bit between. If the light is not of the best, they will still produce leaves with the strong aroma, but the stems will be weaker and the nodes farther apart. We have found no way to make them beauties as to form, but they are sufficiently humble not to be a nuisance.

A large kitchen crop is not to be expected but snippets are constantly finding their way into salads where the characteristic flavor makes up for the small volume. They propagate easily from cuttings and will live a long time. If you are very patient, they may even grow into presentable shrublets.

Origanum vulgare has been naturalized from England all over the Northeast. In August and early September, it forms solid masses of red purple flowers with touches of white. It has larger leaves than the typical oreganos and is a medicinal, not a culinary herb.

A plant of Cretan dittany as it was received from the nursery.
When pinched it starts to branch.

Origanum dictamnus. Dittany of Crete. **Labiatae.** Greece. Perennial.
Culinary aromatic.

The reason why dittany is found more often in herbals than in herb
gardens is that it is a tender plant and just won't take English or American winters. So, again, the indoor grower has the advantage.

   We love our dittany. It is a shrubby little plant with almost round,
thick, silver-woolly leaves. The odor is, surprisingly, pure oregano, but
it is a far prettier plant and easier to grow. Buy a plant and try.

   Grow dittany in small—3- or 4-inch pots—in Lean Mix with plenty
of lime chips. Keep it moist but not soaking and in good light. However,
we find it will tolerate a distance of 12 inches from the tubes and a
position on the side of an east window. Just keep it comfortably house
warm.

   This can be made into a fine specimen plant by careful pruning—
a particularly attractive bonsai. Cuttings of new growth root without
difficulty.

Dittany of Crete has become one of our favorite herbs and never has a chance to grow much because of the cuttings we take for friends. Its velvety grey leaves are beautifully spaced on the branch and the habit of the plant is always graceful. We haven't tried it in cooking but its leaves have a definite oregano-like odor.

Beautiful holly-leaved *Osmanthus.*

Osmanthus. Sweet Olive. **Oleaceae.** China. Perennial. Fragrant flowers.

The sweet olives are shiny-leaved shrubs or small trees that grow up to 20 feet high. Obviously we could not consider them as houseplants were it not that they take very well to drastic pruning and grow very slowly. Also there happens to be a number of dwarf forms. The little white flowers have an intense fragrance of orange. The leaves are shiny and, in some species, much like holly. For many indoor growers this is their favorite fragrant plant.

The most common species is *O. fragrans.* However, the various forms of *O. ilicifolius (aquifolius),* some of which have variegated leaves, are equally desirable. *O. delavayi* is another beauty in this group. Bloom is off and on throughout the year.

Buy neat plants in 4-inch pots and, as they start to grow, keep pruning the tips and shaping. If your sweet olive outgrows its pot, move it to the next size and when it has reached a shape and dimension you like, just keep it that way by trimming the roots each year and keeping the top growth to the same size. Water moderately but never dry out. Use high nitrate fertilizer and, if you have to repot, add Rich Mix. If you have trouble with mites, give it a shower every week for a while.

One of the varieties of Virginia creeper—*Parthenocissus*. With its deep green foliage, touches of red in new growth, and almost yellow reverses of the leaves, it is a most decorative shrubby vine. The berries are a bonus.

Parthenocissus quinquefolia. Virginia Creeper. ***Vitaceae.*** United States Perennial. Medicinal.

Our common Virginia creeper, which appears everywhere in the woods and graces the walls of old houses, holds its leaves well in the house and can be trained as a quite small plant. This is made easier by the existence of some dwarf strains. It's a novelty and at the same time a conversation piece. For, when anyone asks you why you grow it, you can reply that the tea of the leaves taken before liquor will prevent drunkenness. Just boil the bruised leaves and quaff—large mouthfuls at a time, as the herbalists always say. Taken after drinking excessively it will "relieve" drunkenness. What a useful plant to have around the house!

It is also rather pretty, with its shiny "grape" leaves. Just plant it in Rich Mix in nothing bigger than a 4-inch pot, trim it to make it branch, and keep it moist. If you like the idea, hang it in a basket in the window. Use high nitrate fertilizer and propagate by means of tip cuttings.

Plain old maypop. A wildling in the South, this passionflower is very showy and can easily be shrubbed by pruning for indoor growth. Give it your maximum sunlight position and keep rather on the dry side.

Passiflora. Passionflower. *Passifloraceae.* American tropics. Perennial. Medicinal.

In the South *P. incarnata,* called maypop, is a favorite sedative. But the passifloras are principally grown for their complex large flowers in glowing colors. Species and hybrids in white, purple, blue, and red are available from nurseries. In some, the flowers are quite fragrant. For bloom you will probably need a sun porch and grow the plant in a small tub with the stems on a trellis over and around the windows. The effect can be spectacular. The principal other large-flowered types are *P. alato-caerulea, P. caerulea, P. exoniensis, P. coccinea, P. maliformis.* There are quite a few others.

P. *trifasciata* is the most handsome plant for general indoor growing where the flowers are not essential. Whereas the other species have plain green leaves those of *trifasciata* are triple segmented and beautifully patterned in purple and silvery pink. The small yellow flowers are fragrant. This one can be kept small by pruning and makes an unusual foliage plant.

Buy plants and grow in Lean Mix with lime. Fertilize with high phosphate–potash formula and allow to dry out somewhat between waterings. For bloom quite good light is required. It can be done under fluorescent light if the plant can be sufficiently established and the branches kept just below the lights, which is not easy. For plants not grown for bloom, a fair amount of shade is tolerated. Overwatering will produce leaf loss and so will tall growth toward the light leaving behind sections in shade. Unless you have a sun porch or a particularly sunny window, keep the plants pruned back to a small shrub.

149

There are innumerable scented geraniums which differ in leaf form and habit. This plant is a typical example of the *P. crispum,* or lemon-scented, group—probably *P. crispum minor.* Plants are sturdy and durable. The odor is delightful.

Pelargonium hybrids. Scented Geraniums. ***Geraniaceae.*** South Africa and old cultivars. Fragrance.

The garden herbs are principally *P. lancastriense,* which is one of the best blooming herbs, and, to a lesser extent, *P. robertianum,* a pretty wildling. Neither is suitable for the house. The scented geraniums, on the other hand, are recognized as herbs but not grown in the outdoor garden because they are not hardy. As these are a large and interesting group, the indoor gardener has the distinct advantage here.

The leaves of these geraniums are highly scented and, though of little use in the kitchen and of no economic importance for the perfume industry, they provide more different odors than any other plant genus. Collecting scented geraniums is a cult all by itself, and there are those who grow no other plants than these.

The flowers in this group are small and uninteresting but they have the advantage of not requiring dormancy like the flowering kinds and can provide foliage all year round. The worst that happens is that they become woody and don't continue to produce branches anymore—just a case of geriatrics. But by that time you will have had rooting cuttings coming along and new plants.

The leaves are all typically hairy but range from quite simple shapes to ones that look like blown-up snowflakes with lovely lacy lobes with bumps and points. Some of the plants grow tremendously and can be tubbed; others are quite comfortable in a 4-inch pot. In the same way the leaves range in size from a half inch to several inches, from short stalked to very long stalked. The only way to deal with these plants is to do a test run of a collection at a nursery and pick out one or more plants you like. Suppliers all have lists.

The rose geraniums are principally varieties of *P. graveolens* and *P. capitatum*. The best of the lemon-scented are *P. crispum* varieties. *P. crispum minor* has small leaves and strong, bushy growth. 'Dr. Livingston' has 3-inch, wonderfully patterned, lacy leaves with a scent between rose and lemon. *P. grossularioides* and *mellisium* and *P. limoneum* are also strongly aromatic. *P. tomentosum* and *denticulatum* are minty types. And there is a whole gamut of other fragrances including *P. odoratissimum* (apple), *P. scabrum* (apricot), *P. parviflorum* (coconut), *P. concolor* (filbert), *P. torento* (ginger), *P. nervosum* (lime), *P. fragrans* (nutmeg), *P. citriodorum* (orange).

Where old cultivated plants are involved, it has been quite customary to apply species names to variations without any botanical validity. It is probable that not a single one of the above species is entitled to the name but it does identify them after a fashion. In addition, in such a large group as this there are cultivar names, like Dr. Livingston. Add to this, that plants vary from nursery to nursery, and that some of the scents require a strong imagination. So it is best to use your own nose and make your choices on the spot.

Like all geraniums, these prefer it cool but, contrary to the blooming types, will usually tolerate warm temperatures for a time. Use Lean Mix with lime chips and water sparingly. Geraniums really like to be dried out between waterings and won't suffer. They are very much like

A close-up of the lemon-scented geranium.

some begonias in that they can be drooping and recover perfectly once they have been watered. Some require constant pruning, some not. It depends on whether they send out long branches or not. The smaller plants eventually become woody, the larger just go into bigger and bigger pots. They should be rather starved and therefore fertilized with high nitrate solutions only once a month. After all, you aren't asking for a big effort and don't want them to grow fast.

As for light, the fact that we are growing them for leaves makes it possible to raise them without difficulty under lights or in any exposure. We have had some in north light, and poor north light at that, and they have done quite well. They get leggy but if cut back become fairly bushy. The ideal temperature, by the way, is 55° to 65° F.

Petroselinum crispum. Parsley. **Umbelliferae.** Southern Europe and Asia. Biennial. Culinary.

Whatever the name given by the nursery, all the parsleys are variations of *P. crispum.* One type is called Italian parsley—*P. neopolitanum*—and there are numerous other species names that are not necessarily valid. The differences are simply in the fineness or coarseness of the leaves, their curliness or lack of it, vigor of growth and size of roots. Generally speaking, you will buy seeds and take what the seedsman sends you— though garden centers do carry plants in spring. Italian parlsey is stronger flavored and coarser—better for cooking. The curly types are superior for decoration and for salads.

Like all the umbellifers, parsley has a taproot that requires a minimum 4-inch-deep pot. For the same reason it objects to transplanting. These two features, by the way, are why the *Umbelliferae* are such relatively poor houseplants. They belong out in the field like carrots and beets. Soak seed overnight in warm water and plant directly in the pot. It takes five to eight weeks to germinate.

The soil should be ordinary but quite acid. So use Rich Mix without lime and fertilize with high nitrate formulas. Start the seedlings in partial sunlight or directly beneath the tubes. But as they develop, the plants can be removed to partial shade in the sun-room or window and a foot below the tubes. Parsley prefers cool temperatures, dislikes a soggy soil, and should be misted occasionally.

When cutting for use, always remove the outer leaves, not the inner, as growth is from the center. Production should be fair in the house but it is always advisable to keep a couple of pots on the way by seeding every couple of months. A 6-inch pot can hold about five crowded plants.

Typical crisped parsley. Easy to grow but you will need plenty of space to harvest a sufficient amount for daily use.

The looser-leaved Italian-type parsley. Preferred by many for its stronger flavor.

Pretty prunella—a much-neglected plant. One of the loveliest of the low mints.

Prunella vulgaris. Self-heal. ***Labiatae.*** Europe and America. Perennial. Medicinal.

Prunella is a common weed of wayside and meadow. It has rarely been grown, we should think, in any kind of garden. Herbal doctors probably always collected the plant from the wild. We were all the more pleased recently to see it carried, as a garden subject, in a nursery list. For it is a lovely little plant, prettiest of the small labiates, with a constant show of white or pink complex-hooded flowers, forming spikes that are showy relative to the size of the whole plant. Height is 6 to 8 inches in flower. The leaves are shield shaped and plain or toothed. In the house, where scale is so much smaller, prunella is quite big enough and will maintain its bloom all year round, sending up one spike after another, in reflected or fluorescent light.

If you can't find the plant at nurseries, dig it up outdoors. It is a circumpolar species, common everywhere and you will not be transgressing the laws of conservation. At home, pot it in Rich Mix with lime and keep well watered. It needs only occasional fertilizing with high nitrate formula. Since the plant grows by stretching its underground roots, you can maintain it in 4-inch pots and split it whenever it becomes crowded. Cuttings also take easily. It is better to do that than let the flowers go to seed, which might stop the bloom entirely for a while.

Prunella is medicinal all right. It is used as an astringent and is considered useful for sore throats—and healing wounds.

Punica granatum nana. Dwarf Pomegranate. *Punicaceae.* Southern Europe and Asia. Perennial. Medicinal.

We were delighted when, in the process of planning this book, we found out that we could include this superb houseplant among the legitimate herbs. The pomegranate has had a long history of association with religious and magic symbolism but its chief curative property appears to have been as a vermifuge. An infusion of the bark was considered excellent for tapeworm. Among so many herbs that are anything but showy, punica is a standout, compact, free flowering, fruit producing, easy to grow. Even the variety stores often carry the plants.

In the house it is a little, much-branched shrub which, with time, develops a trunk and becomes a one-foot tree. Given an attractive shape, it is a perfect bonsai with its ½-inch, narrow oval, bright green leaves packed close together on the branches. The flowers resemble fuchsias, but are remarkable for having a one-piece large orange calyx which has the texture of a nutshell. From this, the brilliant red orange petals flare out, silky and crumpled. Blow into the flower to pollinate and you may get a fruit about 1½ inches in diameter—a miniature pomegranate—gradually turning a gorgeous red. The seeds are viable, too, though very slow to germinate. It is far easier to propagate from cuttings of the young branches.

We grow it in a maximum 5-inch pot in Rich Mix with plenty of lime. We water it plentifully too and fertilize with anything that's handy. The plant will bloom on the sun porch, in a window facing west or south (perhaps east too) and, under the lights, at a distance of four inches. Start pruning early. Its first branches tend to grow long and weak. Cut back drastically and let a little trunk grow and lots of top branches. Then keep it small by continuous clipping.

Roses are among the few showy garden flowers that have importance in the herb garden. This is a modern mini-rose. It won't provide you with hips for jam but the scent is intense and delicious.

Rosa. Rose. ***Rosaceae.*** Europe and America. Perennial. Fragrance and medicinal.

Wild roses like *R. canina* and *rugosa* are grown for their hips (the seed capsule or fruit) that are high in vitamins, especially C. They are very popular with the organic chompers at present. The rich, unique fragrance of other varieties also makes them herbs. For the house only the miniature roses can be considered.

Nurseries offer many named miniature roses. From these you cannot expect the hips but a few of the plants are as intensely fragrant as a whole plant of tea roses in the garden. There are a number of problems, though, in growing them satisfactorily. They prefer cool conditions like geraniums, in the 55° to 65° F range, and are difficult to keep blooming steadily. They will tolerate high temperatures if treated to the cooling breeze of a fan and not overwatered. But when your first flowers come, you must remove them within a few days. They last a couple of weeks if left alone but if you do that you discourage further bloom. Having removed the flowers you have to cut the plant back, but drastically, right down to main branches and original size. Then you have to wait for more bloom. It's all rather exhausting.

Roses are acid lovers and do best in plain Rich Mix with high nitrate fertilizer and added Sequestrene (chelated iron) if the leaves lose any of their greenness. Keep them moderately watered and give the best light you can in window and in the light garden.

Cuttings, when you trim back, can be used for propagation. Instead of using the propagation box with vermiculite, we take small clear plastic cups; using one of them we fill it with Rich Mix and plant our cutting, the other acts as the cover. Placed in the brightest light you have—right under the fluorescent tubes, for instance—rooting is quite rapid.

The various rosemaries are the easiest pot plants of all the herbs as long as they are kept constantly moist. Their habit is ideal for bonsai treatment, and this specimen is due for a drastic "haircut." It will be cut to half its size and trained. The cuttings make new plants or make an ample supply for the kitchen.

Rosmarinus officinalis. Rosemary. **Labiatae.** Southern Europe. Perennial. Culinary.

Of the culinary herbs, rosemary is the easiest to grow in the house, and it is a nearly perfect foliage shrub. It is half-hardy in this country but in the house it acts like a tender plant, green all the time and growing. The leaves are needlelike, straight or curved, and produced as thickly as pine needles along the woody stems. The odor is intensely pungent and a very few of these leaves is quite enough to flavor lamb or a sauce. The little blue flowers are produced indoors but are of short duration and extremely fragile.

In England a number of named varieties are grown. Here most of the plants are unnamed or merely labeled upright or prostrate, sometimes with the dubious specific name *R. prostratus.* Since rosemary has been grown in so many places and for such a long time, there are many variations in growth habit. It is not true that the prostrate type is easier to grow. We see no difference in this respect among any of them, and our choices are based purely on appearance.

We were curious to see if there were structural differences between some of these rosemaries and discovered any number of ways the little bracts (tiny leaves in the axils of the leaves) appeared. Some were single on either side of the stem, some in twos and threes, some with the three joined together and forming a midget stalk. So the differences go beyond the matter of uprightness or prostration.

We have noted for instance four types of habit. One is erect— probably close to the original *R. officinalis,* with straight leaves and

Rosemary flowers are not showy except when borne in great quantity. They are tiny and typical of the mints.

branches tending to the vertical. Another is more curved in growth—both stem and leaves turn under. The branches grow horizontally. A third looks almost like a dwarf pine tree. The leaves are straight and quite bluish, the growth of the limbs strong. A vigorous-looking plant. This one was labeled *R. prostratus.* A final one is smaller than the others, with very weak, poorly branched stem and very much curled, quite short leaves, a real dwarf. Whatever their habit all can be ruthlessly trimmed and make perfect piny bonsais. All will grow to great age, develop Japanese swirled trunks, and require, to look their best, a substantial tub.

Every book told us to let rosemary dry out between waterings, the theory being that they came from the dry hills of Italy and resented excess moisture. After losing several plants, and having had the experience that some desert plants indoors do best when wet, we started to drown our rosemaries. Result—happy-growing plants and not a problem. We have found that they will almost certainly die if allowed to dry out for a single day. All varieties reacted in the same way.

The soil requirements are Rich Mix with lime. The plants seem to be indifferent to the type of fertilizer and we don't give them much. Once every couple of weeks with a balanced formula is just fine.

Rosemary likes a moderately sunny position but does perfectly well a foot under the lights. House temperatures, hot or cool, do not seem to affect it.

In spite of its woodiness, rosemary cuttings root very fast—sometimes in a matter of a week.

A form of prostrate rosemary which is surprisingly vigorous and greener than most. The habit is horizontal, however, rather than vertical.

A much smaller and slower-growing form of the prostrate rosemary which we found at a nursery.

Still another slow-growing rosemary. This one is unusually silvery and woolly.

The handsome growth and leaves of rue, one of the best herb pot plants for the house.

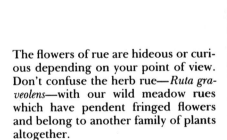

The flowers of rue are hideous or curious depending on your point of view. Don't confuse the herb rue—*Ruta graveolens*—with our wild meadow rues which have pendent fringed flowers and belong to another family of plants altogether.

Ruta graveolens. Rue. **Rutaceae.** Southern Europe. Perennial. Medicinal. Bitter and aromatic.

Rue is a pretty, somewhat tender shrub that is deciduous out of doors and stays green throughout the year in the house. Its sprays of teardrop leaves are bluish in color in some varieties. The flowers are very curious twisted objects with four yellow fringed and cupped petals and a central button. We have never bloomed it in the house but, in spite of their unpleasant odor, we would like to have the flowers just for their oddity.

We have seen rue growing in ditches in Italy and therefore give it Lean Mix with lime, keep it rather moist and set it in our best sun or artificial light. Fertilize only once a month with a balanced formula and prune it to make a shrubby plant.

160

A fine plant of the real herbal sage, *Salvia officinalis* just about ready to flower in a sunny window.

Salvia. Sage. ***Labiatae.*** Europe and Asia. Perennial. Culinary and medicinal.

None of our herbs is more frustrating or puzzling (not even the origanums) than the sages. Herbalist gardeners write about them with a fine abandon but the specimens we have seen in gardens (of the herbal types) were not too well grown and, in the house, they are worse. Some years ago at a flower show a nursery offered greenhouse-grown sages that were absolutely perfect. We would like to know how it was done. We do know that most of the American and English herb garden sages do poorly indoors. We wish we knew more about the Italian and Greek varieties which, because they are more southern, might perform better. Incidentally, it is quite noticeable in Italy that the sage used in cooking is much more delicate than ours, which seems only good for pork and pork sausage.

The sage seeds sold in packages without a qualifying name are supposed to be broad leaved but seem to shrink in the house. We grow them all right but they turn into leggy sprawlers with leaves no more than an inch long. We particularly admire the pimply surface of the leaf and would dearly love to be able to grow fat, broad-leaved plants.

Herb buffs grow all kinds of sages, some of which are culinary, some medicinal, and some just sages. Many come from Mexico and are bushy in habit. This is not necessarily desirable outdoors but is something worthwhile in the house.

We have grown, among others *S. officinalis* and 'Holt's Mammoth.' At a very well kept nursery the latter hardly lived up to its name. In the house it behaved just like the regular *officinalis* and shrank. We have found that besides becoming leggy these sages rapidly become woody, no longer produce leaves lower down the stem, and retain only a cluster at the tips. This may be a shortage of sunlight or artificial light but we are not sure.

Pineapple sage, *S. rutilans,* is great fun because its light green pointed leaves really do smell like the fresh fruit when rubbed. We have

A pot of *Salvia dorisiana,* an attractive compact variety, obviously ready for a larger pot. The leaves lack the "beading" of the true culinary sages.

Holt's Mammoth sage, a tall-growing type with excellent culinary qualities. In the house it should be grown more as a specimen plant. As a hardy sage, it is less adaptable than some of the more southern varieties.

done rather better with that, although the habit of the plant has never been good. In compensation we have been successful in blooming the brilliant scarlet flowers—a much prettier tint than the outdoor salvias of the bedding type. When we show this plant to guests, it always evokes surprise at the first whiff.

An unexpectedly good actor has been *S. officinalis tricolor*. We are not enamored of all those variegations which are so popular but this one is really elegant. The plant is a small shrub with upright purple stems and oval pimpled leaves which are irregularly zoned in green and white (and purple on the new leaves). It has done quite well for us.

These two plants we grow in Rich Mix with lime chips and water rather sparingly. Excess fertilizer seeming merely to encourage excessive growth, we give them a treatment only once a month. The cuttings of both root very quickly in the propagation box with vermiculite.

That is all we can tell you about sage at this time. Hopefully, indoor growers will learn more from experience with them in the next few years, for they are an interesting group of plants which could be most decorative in the house.

A perfect replica of the large sages, this miniature can be kept in shape throughout its long life.

The flowers of *Salvia rutilans*, pineapple sage, are flaming red—among the most beautiful of the herb flowers.

Golden variegated sage. The shape of leaves and the beadings of these types of sage are very attractive. The main problem is to keep them compact in the lower light of the home. Well grown, they are marvelous pot plants.

The sage with the surprising pineapple odor. Still more strange is the way it fades sometimes in the evening and revives in full strength in the morning.

Tricolor sage is one of the handsomest of all herbs. Here is a plant before pruning.

Sanguisorba minor. Salad Burnet. **Rosaceae.** Europe and Asia. Perennial. Culinary.

In the house you won't be able to raise a sufficient crop of salad burnet to feed the family but at least you can experience the flavor and collect enough to make a salad more interestingly tasty. It is one of the few members of the rose family used in the kitchen for its greens. The 15-inch plant has branches with opposite oval leaflets that are deeply indented, and these have a flavor that is nutty and reminiscent of cucumber when used fresh.

Grow a pot of it from seed in well-limed Lean Mix and nip it early in its growth to encourage branching. It will grow nicely in partial sun and should be kept well watered at all times. A section of growing stem tip roots easily. Although this is a perennial, cutting will make a rather misshapen plant with time, so it is a good idea to have plants coming along. The flowers are greenish and quite unattractive. An old salad herb and a novelty in the house.

Exquisite *Santolina incana.* A perfect plant for training and unique for the shape of its foliage.

Santolina chamaecyparissus (incana). Lavender Cotton. **Compositae.** Southern Europe. Aromatic and medicinal.

The santolinas are much grown in herb gardens because of their fine grey foliage, much as are the artemisias. *S. chamaecyparissus* is also called French lavender in spite of the leaves' smelling more like chamomile.

These plants are usually maintained by pruning as low-growing mounds, and their effect in the garden is one of massed contrasting color to the greener herbs. Seeing the foliage from above we have only a confused impression of mistiness and greyness. It is when we bring a single plant into the house that we begin to appreciate lavender cotton fully. For we find that the foliage is not "lacy" but, though extremely fine cut, rather geometrical. Each branchlet, growing from the stems in whorls, bears tiny club-shaped leaves, which give it almost the effect of a square column. Perfectly silvery grey, these leaves catch the light and reflect a gentle glow. The effect is one of a most amazing complex of shapes, rarely found in the plant world. And when it is trained as an individual little shrub in a pot, which is quite easy in this instance, it makes a perfect ornamental miniature.

The variety 'Foxden' is considered particularly grey and feathery. Other species such as *S. virens, pinnata, ericoides,* and *viridis* are greener. Their attraction is in their wild, woody, undisciplined growth. Old plants of *S. virens* look very much like old dwarfed rosemaries. As small specimens they make a beautiful show in the house.

Santolinas will tolerate temperatures in the forties and prefer a rather poor dry soil. Even our Succulent Mix will do for these plants. Out of doors they are treated as annuals but indoors they behave as perennials. Cuttings can be rooted at any time of year.

Santolina pinnata. Some of the santolinas grow beautifully, not as the familiar silvery mounds, but as contorted and decorative-stemmed foliage plants. The long side branches with tiny stiff leaves make a unique pattern.

Santolina virens, one of the green-leaved. Somewhat similar to *pinnata,* it can grow into even wilder and more curious forms—almost like a succulent. These plants are perfect for bonsai.

The tremendous and beautiful flowers of the purple pitcher plant. The leaves drown small insects in water gathered in the cup. Short-stemmed types like this one are easier to bloom in the house than taller ones. Ideal for your indoor herbal bog garden.

Sarracenia purpurea. Pitcher Plant. *Sarraceniaceae.* North America. Perennial. Medicinal.

In a terrarium at least a foot high, sarracenia is an amusing novelty to plant with sundews and butterworts. On the ground, it forms a pinwheel of large hollow leaves with an upright lid and interesting red veining. Both in the window and under fluorescent light, it will bloom in the spring with a single long-stemmed flower which is spectacular—3 inches across with long, hanging purple red petals. When the petals drop off they leave behind a large double-layered green disc which is also very handsome.

Grow sarracenia in moist sphagnum moss and keep the cover of the terrarium closed on all but the hottest days. It should not be fertilized and, if you are tempted to feed it, drop into its mouth only the most minute of insects. It gets indigestion from anything bigger than a match head.

The medicinal uses have been various, but it has been principally used as a tonic.

Satureia montana, winter savory, could be easily mistaken for some of the oreganos, marjorams, and thymes. Often only fine differences of leaf shape and habit differentiate these plants in appearance.

Satureia montana. Winter Savory. ***Labiatae.*** Europe, North Africa. Perennial. Culinary and medicinal.

If any herb can ever be correctly described as hot flavored, then it is certainly savory, which seems to have absorbed all the pungency and suffocating heat of an Italian summer day in the hills. We can vouch for its medicinal value, which is directly related to its culinary uses. For anyone who suffers from the terrible assaults of the bean, savory is a specific. A few dried leaves cooked along with lima, black, or lentil beans will save you from the consequences. It seems to be equally effective against raw cucumber and other gastrically manifested foods. We cheer savory as a benefactor of man and find it surprising that Epicurus, who forbade the eating of beans to his followers, did not discover the herb and let them enjoy these excellent and nutritious vegetables.

Winter savory is a small shrubby herb (to 15 inches) with ½-inch-long needlelike leaves and little, typical mint, flowers in the axils. The related summer savory is an annual. Of the two, this is probably the better tasting. But winter savory will live with you longer and can be propagated from the cuttings as well as divisions. Buy a plant, pot it in Rich Mix with lime, and trim it back so that it will bush. Water moderately. Give it a favored position in the sun or under lights. The fresh herb is more delicate than the dried.

There are a number of forms of winter savory including var. *subspicata*, a creeper, and *S. communis*, an upright form. There are also dwarfs and a so-called var. *grandiflora* which is a bit more showy in bloom than the normal plant.

Labeled by the nurseryman as showy winter savory, this is probably *Satureia calamintha*, calamint, which is often confused with *S. montana*, the true winter savory, which has narrow leaves. This is a prettier plant and grows well in the house.

A baby tamarind tree with its pot standing on a square of plastic egg crate. Tamarinds can be trained as bushy, shapely houseplants.

Tamarindus indica. Tamarind. ***Leguminosae.*** Africa and South Asia. Medicinal and in flavoring.

The tamarind tree grows to 80 feet in the tropics and bears yellow flowers followed by the long pods associated with trees of the bean family. Clean or eat the tart flesh from the bean, soak in water overnight, and plant in a small pot in Rich Mix with lime. The cotyledons (bean halves) are shoved up out of the soil to a height of three inches and the leaves then open up rather spectacularly. They are, at the start, 3 to 4 inches long and consist of many oval leaflets.

After the third pair of leaves appears, remove them, forcing the plant to put out side branches. From then on, keep pruning unless you want a big showy plant for the window. We have one that was 12 feet long and stretched right across most of a triple window but which we cut back to 4 feet. There it stays without further pruning except for some side branches that get out of hand occasionally. The appearance is very attractive because of the fineness of the leaves. The leaves, by the way, fold up in pairs at night as do those of other trees of this family.

Thus a tamarind may be kept moderately small—no more than a foot high or grown into a big specimen plant. In the latter case it must be moved to larger pots as it grows. It is a very thirsty plant and does not mind standing in water as long as the temperature stays above 68° F. Fertilize it with a balanced solution with every watering. The only other thing to watch out for is mite which can strip the leaves rather rapidly. Since this is not a plant we use directly in cooking, you can hang a No-Pest Strip among the branches and spray thoroughly with water at least once a week. Without other care it provides beautiful greenery for years. This is one of the tropical plants that will soon begin to replace the rather coarse avocado in our homes.

171

Taraxacum officinale. Dandelion. ***Compositae.*** Europe and America. Perennial. Culinary and medicinal.

Surprise your friends by growing an authentic nuisance weed in the house. There are few plants that will arouse a stronger reaction like "Why on earth are you growing that thing?" This alone is a good reason for having a pot around. But it has long been a valued salad and medicinal herb, too.

We have a special affection for the dandelion. It strengthened our thumb and index fingers in our early days as we plucked away to clear the lawn. Later we used a forked instrument, which was less fun, and now we commit dandelionicide with herbicides, which isn't fair at all.

The young leaves are the best of all the salad greens—bitter, clean-flavored, and ideal to mix in with the more insipid lettuces to which it is so closely related botanically. Formerly, Italian immigrant ladies would scour the lawns of everybody for these weeds but whether they were seeking their medicinal or edible parts we do not know. Possibly the former, for its root has long been used as a stomachic and tonic.

We have recently seen the seeds listed in a herbal catalogue, and paying for them would probably add to the fun. But it is quite a simple matter to dig up a very young plant and move it to a deep pot—at least a 4-incher—and give it any kind of poor soil or Lean Mix. Water it well and set it in partial sun and you may be rewarded with flowers. Pick the outside leaves for your salad.

Teucrium chamaedrys. Germander. ***Labiatae.*** Europe. Perennial. Medicinal.

We are particularly amused at growing the medicinal herbs that were formerly renowned for treating gout, which is now a rather unusual ailment due to somewhat different, though not necessarily better, drinking habits. However, if you have germander handy you can always treat that rare case—at your own risk.

Germander is a pretty shrublet, growing up to a foot, which will perhaps flower for you in the house, rosy or bright red. The *Labiatae* are thus named because of their two-lipped tube form. In some members of the family, the upper part is the most prominent, or they are even, or the lower lip is much larger. In Teucrium the lower lip is very much enlarged and angles downward.

The leaves are almost stalkless, opposite, hairy, and toothed. The habit is neat, upright, and compact. Grow it in a 3- or 4-inch pot in limy Rich Mix and give it moderate sunlight and even moisture.

Teucrium canadense grows all over the eastern part of the United States and is a steeple type of plant with a long inflorescence and purple dotted whitish flowers. It is reputed to be a "stimulant, aromatic and bitter." It is worth mentioning here because plants grow well south of the frost line in Florida and should do well in the house. But it is an altogether bigger, coarser plant than *T. chamaedrys*.

Cuttings of both will root easily but it is advisable to start with a plant. Wild flower nurseries usually carry the American germander.

Teucrium germander, properly *T. chamaedrys,* has small attractive leaves, many stems growing from the base and an erect habit. This adds up to a very easy plant to shape for beauty in the home. It is easy to divide the plants when they grow too large for the pot.

Thymus citriodorus. Related to *T. vulgaris,* this plant illustrates the broader rounded leaf of the type. It can sprawl like all the other thymes.

Thymus. Thyme. **Labiatae.** Europe, North Africa. Perennial. Culinary and medicinal.

The thyme complex is the most complex of the complex culinary herbs. Except for the true species, which also vary considerably depending on where they have been grown for a long time, the plants receive their names rather willfully, according to what the nurseryman smells or tastes. The English have named varieties that run fairly true to type at least in plants if not in seed. These northern plants, especially the ones grown here for their hardiness, are the least interesting for the indoor gardener. Our best thymes are from southern countries.

The typical thyme odor is sweleringly hot, like savory, only more appetizing. The typical plant is a sprawling shrublet with ½-inch, very narrow, numerous leaves and upright short spikes of pink flowers. It is a favorite garden ground cover which can be trodden on without serious damage. All over the eastern United States, *T. serpyllum* grows in lawns, and in the Catskills there are open mountainsides carpeted with it—a populous immigrant. This also indicates thyme's favorite position —full sun in poor, gravelly, well-drained soil, though it is pretty versatile and will also flourish where the soil is richer and damper. We use Lean Mix with double the recommended quantity of lime chips, and we water sparingly. Lime chips are better than powdered lime because they approximate gravel while neutralizing the soil.

In the house, thyme is often not too happy because of the need for

With its training begun, this lemon thyme is standing erect.

sun but, with care, it can be grown nicely and we have even seen this same *T. serpyllum* spreading far and wide under fluorescent light. The plants vary so much that a certain amount of luck is involved. And when you have a plant that behaves, propagate it by stem cuttings and plant several to a pot. On the whole it is advisable to allow some drying out between waterings.

The odors of thymes vary from rather faint to very strong, from typical to all kinds of interesting or unattractive ones that are more or less lemony, fruity, bitter, and so on. So, here again, it is a matter of picking plants at a nursery. Seeds rarely work out as well; there are too many different thymes and too many home environments to trust the seed package. Far better to pick out a few plants (they are small in any event) and continue to grow and propagate those that suit you best.

T. serpyllum, the thyme most used in England, has many horticultural forms, some of which are difficult to tell apart even by experts.

Thymus lanuginosus is a very woolly plant that has somewhat more substance than the other thymes. An older plant makes a beautiful little furry shrub.

A good example of how *not* to grow *Thymus serpyllum*. This delicious thyme is a natural straggler, gradually developing a bushy structure. Grow in wide shallow pots with plenty of lime chips and keep trimming until you have a neat woody plant. The leaves of all the thymes are so tiny that it is difficult to grow a crop in the house.

Naturalized everywhere in the East, on lawns and mountain mead-
ows, *Thymus serpyllum* makes an exquisite ground cover and, for its
size, provides a charming flower display.

Individual ones may do well in the house but obviously we cannot try
them all. Most, however, are too hardy for our purposes. All kinds of
variations turn up, fuzzy leaves, lemon odored, yellowish leaves, variegation. We don't find that in so small a plant variegation means much.
Collecting a quantity of such small leaves is a headache. Even in the
aforementioned Catskills, surrounded by the plants, we have had difficulty clearing enough leaves to load a sandwich. The commercial herb
driers must have their secret methods of handling large quantities.

T. vulgaris is a more southerly plant and more shrubby, therefore
better for us. Leaves are small but, being a bit upright, it makes a
finer-looking plant in the house. Here too there are lemony and variegated plants.

With time (no pun implied), nurserymen, instead of gathering only
the more hardy plants for the outdoor garden, will start to carry more
varieties from the Mediterranean and North Africa—plants far more
suitable for us. Among these possibilities are *T. broussonettii* from
Morocco, *T. carnosus* from Portugal, T. *glabrescens* from Greece, *T. nitidus*
from Sicily, *T. hyemalis* from Spain, *T. zygis* from Sicily. An interesting
sturdy plant which is available is *T. herba-barona* from Corsica. You may
find others if you search the nursery lists.

Thymus vulgaris argenteus. This young plant is ready to be cut back to the cluster at the bottom. It will branch more then and develop a bushy growth. Only then will the massing of variegated leaves make a good show.

Compact varieties of nasturtium grow well in small pots indoors, and provide both beautiful flowers and tasty greens.

Tropaeoleum majus. Nasturtium. *Tropaeolaceae.* South America. Annual. Culinary.

Being peppery, nasturtium leaves are one of those greens we add to salads to give them life and flavor (iceberg lettuce is enough to drive anyone to herbs). The seeds may be used like capers after being pickled in vinegar, salt, and pepper.

The big varieties are growable in a particularly well lighted sun porch where they have plenty of room to climb or hang. For less favorable positions use the dwarf and bush types, giving them the best light you can. A Rich Mix will produce more leaves, and with a Lean Mix you may have more flowers. Water sparingly and fertilize not more than once a week. If you plant seeds every couple of months you can have the leaves throughout the year.

Aphids are very partial to nasturtiums and eggs often come with the seeds. Catch them early, and you can wash them off with soap flakes if you are planning to eat the leaves. Later on spray with nicotine sulphate (Black Flag).

Vinca major and **minor.** Periwinkle. ***Apocynaceae.*** Europe and Asia. Perennial. Medicinal.

For the indoor grower it is helpful to find that vinca is a herb. It's useful in hemorrhages. *V. rosea,* a South African species, is reported by Potter to be a better cure for diabetes than insulin. If that is the case, let's go into business.

Periwinkle is a most common plant in settled places along our roadsides where it takes refuge in a smooth shady place and lights up the darkness with its pure blue flowers, sometimes white or pink. It is a perfect ground cover for a difficult damp spot in the shade as far as survival is concerned, though the plain dark leaves are not too attractive.

The same qualities that make it unsuitable for most herb gardens, which lie out in the sun, offers an advantage to the indoor gardener. In the house it grows nicely and its blue flowers look much larger.

Give it a Rich Mix without lime, plenty of water, and a high nitrate fertilizer. It will do well on the side of a window or back of a sun porch. Under lights it tends to spread over the pot but can either be treated as a hanging plant or clipped back so that it has short branches. Propagate by cuttings.

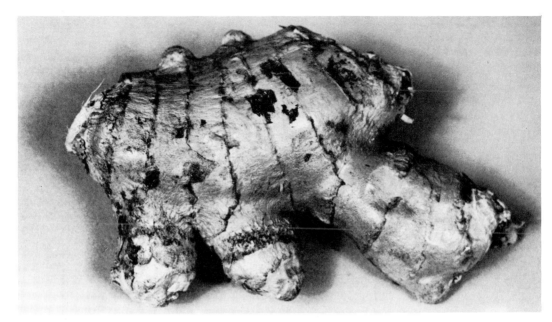

A typical healthy piece of ginger root. Plant it and you will have both greenery and a lot of additional root.

Zingiber officinale. Ginger. ***Zingiberaceae.*** China. Perennial. Culinary, medicinal, and fragrant.

At the other end of the alphabet from *Alpinia* is its relative in the family, the real ginger. Although we use it plentifully in our cooking, we can't help thinking of it as a geriatric stomachant, because grandma lived on Jamaica ginger which soothed her distresses. Of course it is also a valuable spice. The leaves are gently gingerish and aromatic—good in soup. It is fun to grow ginger indoors because it is the only herb from which you get a root crop except onion.

All you do is start with a piece of root bought from a Chinese or Japanese grocery. Don't choose the largest piece in the place. A couple of inches are enough, but that should be fresh and fat. Roots that have been exposed to freezing in the winter will not grow for you.

Plant with the top just below the surface of the soil, in Rich Mix in an azalea pot. Leave room for spread. Moisten but do not soak the soil and put the pot in a warm closet until shoots appear. Then it can be brought to the best light you have.

Although ginger has attractive flowers, which grow in club-shaped growths from the base, you are more likely to settle for the clustered stems of long-leafed grass very much like *Amomum cardamon,* only somewhat narrower. If the leafy growth is healthy, the tuber will start to spread and, before you know it, will fill the whole interior of the pot. At that point you can remove the root and report it or cut off a small piece for propagation and use the rest in the kitchen. The ginger is perfectly real and tasty—good for candying or grating in your cooking. Give the plant high nitrate fertilizer and keep it moist when the light is good and a little on the dry side when it isn't. Warmth over 65° and high humidity encourage growth.

Bibliography

ARBER, AGNES. *Herbals, Their Origin and Evolution.* Darien, Conn.: Hafner Publishing Company, 1970.

BROWNLOW, MARGARET. *Herbs and the Fragrant Garden.* New York: McGraw-Hill Book Company, 1963.

CLARKSON, ROSETTA E. *The Golden Age of Herbs and Herbalists.* Dover. Publications, Inc.

_____. *Herbs and Savory Seeds.* New York: Dover Publications, Inc.

DASTUR, J. F. *Medicinal Plants of India and Pakistan.* Bombay, India: D. P. Taraporevala Sons & Company Ltd.

FOX, HELEN M. *Gardening with Herbs for Flavor and Fragrance.* New York: Dover Publications, Inc.

_____. *The Years in My Herb Garden.* New York: Macmillan Company.

GRIEVE, M. *Culinary Herbs and Condiments.* New York: Dover Publications, Inc.

_____. *A Modern Herbal.* 2 Vols. New York: Dover Publications, Inc.

Handbook on Herbs. Brooklyn Botanic Garden Vol. 14.

HATTO, RICHARD G. *Handbook of Plant and Floral Ornament from Early Herbals.* New York: Dover Publications, Inc., 1960.

HOGNER, DOROTHY Childs. *A Fresh Herb Platter.* Garden City, N.Y.: Doubleday & Company, Inc.

KAMM, MINNIE W. *Old Time Herbs from Northern Gardens.* New York: Dover Publications, Inc.

LOEWENFELD, CLAIRE. *Herb Gardening.* London: Faber and Faber.

MEYER, JOSEPH E. *The Herbalist.* Issued by Clarence Meyer.

MILORADOVICH, MILO. *The Art of Cooking with Herbs and Spices.* New York: Doubleday & Company, Inc., 1954.

NORTHCOTE, LADY ROSALIND. *The Book of Herb Lore.* New York: Dover Publications, Inc.

PATERSON, CATHERINE CHILDS. *Medieval Gardens.* New York: Hacker Art Books, 1966.

RHODE, ELEANOR SINCLAIR. *A Garden of Herbs.* New York: Dover Publications, Inc.

———. *Herb and Herb Gardening.* London: Medici Society.

———. *Rose Recipes from Olden Times.* New York: Dover Publications, Inc.

SIMMONS, ADELMA GRENIER. *Herbs to Grow Indoors.* New York: Hawthorn Books, Inc., 1969.

SPRY, CONSTANCE. *Constance Spry Cooking Book.* London: J. M. Dent.

WOODWARD, MARCUS. *Leaves from Gerard's Herbal.* New York: Dover Publications, Inc.

USDA Agriculture Handbook No. 249. Elbert L. Little, Jr. and Frank H. Wadsworth. *Common Trees of Puerto Rico and the Virgin Islands.* 1964.

WREN, R. C. *Potter's Cyclopaedia of Botanical Drugs and Preparations.* London: Potter and Clarke, Ltd., 1932.

Sources for Herb Plants and Seeds

Almost all seedsmen with catalogs containing flower and vegetable seeds also carry herbs—usually as a seed listing. However, few of these mail order suppliers give any detailed information about the seeds or specify the variety so that you can find out about it in a book on herb gardening. With luck you may receive a very good strain of a herb in your seed packet. But results are by no means uniform, and one major seedsman even sells tarragon seed without specifying that it is not the true culinary tarragon. This happens because herb seeds are a staple of the business, and the seedsman himself, when he buys his supplies, probably asks few questions regarding the plants that will grow from these seeds. His main concern is that the seed be capable of sprouting. Plants are much more reliable—even by mail order.

Ashby's Garden Centre & Nursery, Cameron, Ontario, Canada. Plants. List 20¢.
Barr, Claude. Prairie Gem Ranch, Smithwick, S. Dak. 57782. Seeds.
Black Forest Botanicals, Route 1, Box 34, Yuba, Wis. 54672. Catalog 10¢.
Bluemont Nurseries, P. O. Box 219, Monkton, Md. 21111. Wholesale plants.
Borchelt Herb Gardens, East Falmouth, Mass. 012536. Catalog 15¢.
Burpee, W. Atlee, Co., Hunting Park Ave. at Eighteenth St., Philadelphia, Pa. 19132. Seeds.
Calumet Herb Company, P. O. Box 248, South Holland, Ill. 60473.
Cape Cod Nurseries, P. O. Drawer B., Falmouth, Mass. 02541
Caprilands Herb Farm, Coventry, Conn. 06238. Plants and Seed. Several lists.
Carobil Farm, Church Road, Brunswick, Maine 04011. Plants.
Carroll Gardens, Westminster, Md. 21157. Excellent catalog 50¢.

Cedarbrook Herb Farm, Sequim, Wash. 98382. List 10¢.

Central Nursery Company, 2675 Johnson Avenue, San Luis Obispo, Calif. 93401. Seeds.

Chientan & Co., 1001 S. Alvarado St., Los Angeles, Calif. 90006. Chinese herbs.

Chong Shay Herb Co., 1057 S. Main, Los Angeles, Calif. 90015. Chinese herbs.

Chong's Nursery and Flowers, P. O. Box 2154, Honolulu, Hawaii 96805.

Comstock, Ferre & Co., Wethersfield, Conn. 06109.

Cottage Herb Farm Shop, 311 State St., Albany, N.Y. 12210. Catalog 10¢.

Edmund's Native Plant Nursery, 2190 Oak Grove Road, Walnut Creek, Calif. 94589

Exeter Wildflower Gardens, Exeter, N.H. 03883. Wholesale plants.

Ferndale Nursery, Akov, Minn. 55704. Native herbs.

Frog Meadow Herb Farm, Washington Depot, Conn. 06794. Plants and seeds.

Gardens of the Blue Ridge, Ashford, N.C. 28603. Native wild herbs.

Greene Herb Gardens, Greene, R.I. 02898. Dried herbs, seeds, plants. List.

Gurney Seed Co, Yankton, S.D. 59078.

Harris, Joseph, Co., Moreton Farm, Rochester, N.Y. 14624. Plants.

Hart Seed Co., Wethersfield, Conn. 06109. Seed.

Hemlock Hill Herb Farm, Litchfield, Conn. 06759. Plants. Catalog 25¢.

Herb Farm, The., Barnard Road, Granville, Mass. 01034. Plants, dried herbs.

Herb House, The., P. O. Box 308. Beaumont, Calif. 92223. Catalog 15¢.

Herb Store, The., Sherman Oaks, Calif. 91403. Catalog 25¢.

Hilltop Herb Farm, P. O. Box 866, Cleveland, Tex. 77327. Catalog 30¢.

Hindue East Indian Herb Co., 635 W. Court, Cincinnati, Ohio 45203.

House of Herbs, 459 Eighteenth Avenue, Newark, N.J. 07108.

Hudson, J. L., P. O. Box 1058, Redwood City, Calif. 04064. Seed. Catalog 50¢.

Hurov's Tropical Tree Nursery, P. O. Box 10387, Oahu, Honolulu, Hawaii 96813. Plants and seeds.

Jamicson Valley Gardens, Route 3, Spokane, Wash. 99203. Plants.

Leodar Nurseries, 7206 Belvedere Road, West Palm Beach, Fla. 33406. Plants and seeds.

Leslie's Wildflower Nursery, 30 Summer Street, Methuen, Mass. 01884. Herb plants. Catalog 20¢.

Logee's Greenhouses, 55 North Street, Danielson, Conn. 06239. Plants. Catalog 50¢.

Lounsberry Gardens, Oakford, Ill. 62673. Plants. Catalog 25¢.

Mail Box Seeds, 2042 Encinal Avenue, Alameda, Calif. 94501. Seeds. List 50¢.

Merry Gardens, Camden, Maine 04843. Plants. Catalog 25¢.

Mincemoyer Nursery, Box 482, Jackson, N.J. 08527. Plants.

Murchie's, 1008 Robson St., Vancouver 105, British Columbia, Canada. Catalog 25¢.

Nichols Garden Nursery, 1190 N. Pacific Highway, Albany, Oreg. 97321. Plants and seeds.

Oakhurst Gardens, Arcadia, Calif. 91006. Plants. Catalog 50¢.

Orchid Gardens, Box 224, Grand Rapids, Mich. 55744. Plants. Catalog 25¢.

Park, George W., Seed Co., Greenwood, S.C. 29646. Seed.

Payne, Theodore, Foundation, 10459 Tuxford St., Sun Valley, Calif. 91352. Plants. Catalog 50¢.

Penn Herb Co., 603 N. Second St., Philadelphia, Pa. 19123.

Putney Nursery, Putney, Vt. 05346. Plants. Catalog 25¢.

Richter, Otto, & Sons Ltd., Locust Hill, Ontario, Canada. Catalog 50¢.

Robin, Clyde. P. O. Box 2091 Castro, Calif. 94546. Herbs and herb seeds. Catalog $1.

Rocky Hollow Herb Farm, Sussex, N.J. 07461. Plants. Catalog 50¢.

Rosemary House, The. Mechanicsburg, Pa. 17055. Catalog 25¢.

Roth, H., & Son, 1577 First Avenue, New York, N.Y. 10028. Catalog.

Shop in the Sierra. P. O. Box 1, Midpines, Calif. 95345. Catalog 25¢.

Shuttle Hill Herb Shop, Delmar, N.Y. 12054. Catalog 25¢.

Siskiyou Rare Plant Nursery, Medford, Oreg. 97501.

Springbrook Gardens, 6776 Heisley Road, Mentor, Ohio 44060. Wholesale plants. Catalog.

Stoke Lacy Herb Farm, Bromyard, Herefordshire, England. Seeds for import.

Sunnybrook Herb Farm Nursery, Mayfield Road, Chesterfield, Ohio 44026 Plants. Excellent catalog 25¢.

Taylor's Garden, 2649 Stingle Ave., Rosemead, Calif. 91770. Plants.

Thompson & Morgan, Seedsmen, Ipswich, England. Catalog. Send $2.00.

The Tool Shed, North Salem, N.Y. 12865. Plants. Catalog 25¢.

Vick's Wild Gardens, Gladwyne, Pa. 19035. Native herbs.

Wayside Gardens, Mentor, Ohio 44060. Plants. Catalog $2.00.

White Flower Farm, Litchfield, Conn. 06759. Plants. Catalog $2.00.

Wild Garden, The. P. O. Box 487, Bothell, Wash. 98011.

Plant Societies

For information on all aspects of indoor gardening join the
Indoor Light Gardening Society of America, Inc.
C/o Mrs. James C. Martin, 423 Powell Drive, Bay Village,
Ohio 44140. Annual dues $5.00.
Bimonthly magazine *Light Garden*, Round Robins, Seed Fund.
Chapters in major cities.

Index

190